Table of Contents

Chapter 1

Introduction:

In 1971, Orlando was put on the map as the theme park destination capital of the world with the opening of the Walt Disney World Resort and Magic Kingdom Park – it was a place where families could visit together to make memories and dreams came true every day. The resort was a giant version of the Disneyland Resort that Walt Disney opening in 1955.

Much like Disney, in the late 1980s, Universal thought it would get in on the thrill game too by opening its own East-coast theme park, similar to that which it had opened in 1965 in Hollywood but on a bigger scale. Universal made the announcement that it would be bringing its own theme park to Orlando much to the delight of locals.

Disney soon saw that this new theme park could be a big competitor and decided that it too would build a theme park based around studios, then dubbed Disney's MGM Studios. Miraculously, Disney's MGM Studios managed to open its doors in 1989 before the grand opening of Universal Studios Florida one year later. MGM was a rushed project, and when Universal Studios Florida opened its blew Disney's MGM Studios out of the water in terms of the quality and standard of attractions.

In 1995, the expansion of Universal Orlando began as the company invested billions of dollars to create a second theme park – *Universal's Islands of Adventure*. Three on-site resort hotels and an entertainment and dining district, *CityWalk,* were also constructed. The original Universal Studios Florida park was also expanded with new areas – the aim was to create a multi-day destination that would rival Disney.

On May 28 1999, *Universal's Islands of Adventure* opened to rave reviews with innovative attractions such as *The Amazing Adventures of Spiderman* and *The Incredible Hulk Coaster* winning awards year after year, even to this day. (Side note: In our opinion *Hulk* is still the best coaster in all of Florida)

With this expansion, Universal moved into the mouse's territory – it was no longer just a theme park. Universal Orlando became a veritable destination – a place to spend multiple days on-site, to explore themed adventures and to create memories that last a lifetime.

The Universal Orlando Resort has fast become *the* place to visit in Orlando - the opening of innovative attractions and lands such as *The Simpsons Ride, The Wizarding World of Harry Potter, Hollywood Rip Ride Rockit* and *Transformers: The Ride* have sent the visitor figures skyrocketing. Collectively, both theme parks now welcome over 16 million guests per year.

By the time you have finished reading this travel guide you will know all about your dining options, which attractions to do and which to miss, how to save hours in queue lines, where to stay, tips on how to save money and time, seasonal events, the future of the theme parks, and about all the services the parks offer. With this guide you can do all this important research before you have even set foot into the parks - you will truly be ahead of the game.

Universal Orlando is an unforgettable vacation destination - you will make memories that last a lifetime. 2016 marks an exciting year for the resort with a new resort hotel opening and the long-awaited King Kong attraction – there has never been a better time to visit.

Contact us:

If you have any questions about this travel guide or the Universal Orlando Resort please contact us via the contact form on our website at **www.independentguidebooks.com** and we will be happy to assist before, during and after your trip. Also be sure to subscribe to our newsletter on the right hand side of the website for updates from us.

Limit of Liability and Disclaimer of Warranty:

The publisher has used its best efforts in preparing this book, and the information provided herein is provided "as is." Independent Guides and the author make no representation or warranties with respect to the accuracy or completeness of the contents of this book and specifically disclaims any implied warranties of merchantability or fitness for any particular purpose and shall in no event be liable for any loss of profit or any other commercial damage, including but not limited to special, incidental, consequential, or other damages. Please read all signs before entering attractions, as well as the terms and conditions of any companies' services which you use. Food prices are approximate, and do fluctuate.

COPYRIGHT NOTICE:

Chapter 2

Tickets:

Getting the right Universal Orlando ticket is crucial and it can save you a lot of money. There are many different ticket options that can be purchased for Universal Orlando. In this section we dissect them all.

Advanced Tickets

Advanced tickets can be bought by all guests from anywhere around the world. The easiest place to purchase these tickets is the official Universal Orlando website at www.universalorlando.com. There are two types of advanced tickets: single-park tickets which allow you access to one theme park per day (either to *Universal Studios Florida* or *Islands of Adventure* on any one day), or park-to-park tickets which allow you to enter both theme parks and go back and forth between them.

With multi-day single park tickets you are able to visit the two parks on separate days but you will not be able to visit both parks on the same day (for that you would need a park-to-park ticket) – single park tickets allow you to ride every attraction in a single park per day with the exception of the *Hogwarts Express* attraction which requires a park-to-park ticket.

As you will see from the prices below, a single day ticket is expensive on its own. The second day is about half the price of the first day and additional days cost only $10 extra per day.

Park-to-park tickets are $45 more expensive than single park tickets, regardless of the length of the ticket. You need to think carefully about whether the flexibility of moving between parks on the same day, and access to the *Hogwarts Express* attraction are worth the extra cost.

Child prices apply to children aged 3 to 9 years old. Children under 3 get free admission into the theme parks (proof of age may be requested at the turnstiles). Note that prices below exclude tax.

Single Park Tickets:

	1 Day	2 Days	3 Days	4 days
Adult	$102	$149.99	$159.99	$169.99
Child	$97	$139.99	$149.99	$159.99

Park-to-Park tickets:

	1 Day	2 Days	3 Days	4 days
Adult	$147	$194.99	$204.99	$214.99
Child	$142	$184.99	$194.99	$204.99

Advanced tickets are e-tickets that can either be picked up from will-call kiosks at the theme parks, or printed at home saving you valuable vacation time. Alternatively, you can have your tickets shipped to you in the mail. Multi-park tickets bought online include a coupon book with $150 worth of savings. A Universal "convenience fee" of $2.15 for booking in advance will also be added to any booking made online. Physical tickets will be shipped out via FedEx at an additional cost – we recommend you print your own tickets at home or use the 'Will Call' option to save on postage fees.

Top Tip: With the exception of 1-Day tickets, all other **tickets are $20 more expensive per person at the park gates** (you will be able to see this 'gate' pricing in the next section). So book online and save yourself some serious cash and time. The 'Will Call' machines at the front of the park are only to pick up advanced purchase tickets. If you have not purchased in advance, expect a long wait in the ticket queue line to see a Team Member to buy your tickets.

Top Tip 2: You can buy tickets at your on-site hotel; you will save $20 on your multi-day tickets compared to park prices meaning that you pay the same price as is charged online.

Top Tip 3: Universal does not have its own water park but you can add access to the great 'Wet and Wild' water park which is located just across the road. This add-on can be purchased on multi-day tickets – one visit is $35 or up to 14 days' entry can be purchased for $55. Universal will be closing down 'Wet and Wild' on 1st January 2017 and will open its own water park later in 2017.

Top Tip 4: If you are enjoying the resort so much that you want to add extra days onto your ticket, be sure to visit Guest Relations at the park before the last day expires. Here an extra day can be added for as little as $10 per ticket – making adding an extra day onto a trip very affordable indeed.

Top Tip 5: Be sure to ask your work HR department whether they are part of the Universal Fan Club. Membership is free but registration is only open to companies. HR can register by emailing **fanclub@universalorlando.com** - you will benefit from slightly discounted tickets and other offers.

Top Tip 6: The prices stated above are the ticket prices from the official Universal Orlando website. There are other websites and ticket brokers available that may offer tickets at further reduced prices. We recommend you thoroughly check the reputation of the website you are purchasing from if you are not ordering from the official Universal website. Avoid auctions and second-hand sales.

Gate Price Tickets:

If you do not purchase your tickets in advance, you will need to purchase them at the theme park entrance ticket booths – these are "gate price" tickets and are by far the most expensive. The price of a one-day ticket is the same online or at the gate.

All multi-day tickets are $20 more expensive when purchased at the theme park. In addition to paying over the odds, you will waste valuable vacation time by getting in a queue line when you could have been enjoying the theme parks instead. As you have this guide and are clearly planning your Universal Orlando vacation in advance, there is no excuse for having to buy a ticket at the gate.

Single Park Tickets:

	1 Day	2 Days	3 Days	4 days
Adult	$102	$169.99	$179.99	$189.99
Child	$97	$159.99	$169.99	$179.99

Park-to-Park tickets:

	1 Day	2 Days	3 Days	4 days
Adult	$147	$214.99	$224.99	$234.99
Child	$142	$204.99	$214.99	$224.99

Top Tip: A disability discount of 15% off the gate price is available, meaning savings of over $35 on a 4-day park-to-park adult ticket. This is also applicable to members of the family who feel they will not be able to experience all the attractions in the park perhaps due to fear or age requirements. Tickets must be bought on the day from Guest Services.

No proof of disability is required – remember this is a generous discount; please do not abuse it as it could be withdrawn at any time. Some tickets will still be cheaper online than at the park gates with this discount. You may also decide that even if there are extra savings to be had, you would rather pay full price online and not queue up on the day of your visit.

Top Tip: All multi-day tickets are $20 cheaper than the prices above when purchased in advance online.

UK tickets:

Residents of the United Kingdom usually visit Florida for a longer period of time period than American visitors, so naturally Universal offers different and longer ticketing options. These "Universal Bonus Tickets" must be purchased in the UK before departing for the US, as they are not available outside the UK.

2016 pricing for a 2-park bonus ticket with access to both Universal theme parks for 14 consecutive days is priced at £149 for adults and £142 for children. A 3-park bonus ticket with access to both Universal theme parks (plus access to Wet 'n Wild) for 14 consecutive days is priced at £164 for adults and £157 for children.

Florida Resident Tickets:

Florida Residents can take advantage of discounts on multi-day tickets. Proof of residency must be shown when picking up tickets and/or when entering the turnstiles. Florida residents who are planning on visiting for more than 3 days in a year should also strongly consider the Universal Orlando annual passes.

A valid Florida ID must be shown for each ticket purchased when picking them up. Accepted IDs are:

- Florida driver's license
- Florida state-issued ID card (must have Florida address)
- Florida voter's registration card with corresponding photo ID
- College ID from a Florida college or university with corresponding photo ID

Florida Resident Single Park Tickets:

	1 Day	2 Days	3 Days
Adult	$102	$132.99	$142.99
Child	$97	$123.99	$133.99

Florida Resident Park to Park tickets:

	1 Day	2 Days	3 Days
Adult	$147	$166.99	$176.99
Child	$142	$157.99	$167.99

As well as being cheaper than standard tickets, the multi-park tickets are valid for up to 60 days meaning that you have added flexibility as to when you can visit. Florida Resident discounted tickets must be purchased online in advance and then collected at any ticket window at both theme parks – these tickets cannot be purchased at the gates.

Blackout dates apply to Florida resident tickets. These are: Dec 18th 2015 to Jan 2nd 2016; March 19th, 2016 to April 2nd, 2016; June 11th, 2016 to August 15th, 2016; and December 17th, 2016 to December 31st, 2016.

Annual Passes

Annual passes allow you to visit the resort as often as you wish (subject to blackout dates on some passes) at a very low per-visit price. In addition, special perks are offered to Passholders including discounts on dining and merchandise. There are three types of annual pass available. Discover them all below.

	Power Pass	Preferred Pass	Premier Pass
Pricing	$239.99	$334.99	$479.99
A year of unlimited park to park admission	No. Blockout dates apply.	Yes	Yes
Free self-parking (after first visit)	No	Yes	Yes
Free valet and preferred self-parking	No	No	Yes
Discounts on theme park and special event tickets	No	Yes	Yes
One Free (non-peak) Halloween Horror Nights Ticket	No	No	Yes
Free admission to select special events	Yes	Yes	Yes
Discounted food, merchandise and specialty items	No	Yes (10% off both food and merchandise)	Yes (15% off food and 20% off merchandise)
Discount on	Yes	Yes	Yes

Blue Man Group Tickets			
Free CityWalk club access	No	No	Yes
Discounts at on-site hotels	Yes	Yes	Yes
Universal Express Pass access (after 4:00pm – once per participating ride)	No	No	Yes
8 bottles of free water	No	No	Yes

Prices are exclusive of tax. Prices are the same for all guests regardless of age. Restrictions apply to some of these benefits.

Top Tip: If you are visiting the resort for over 4 days it makes sense to purchase the 'Preferred Pass' for one member of your family, and regular park tickets for the others. The pass will give you food and merchandise discounts, as well as free regular self-parking, meaning it will likely quickly pay for itself.

Top Tip 2: Remember if you are planning two multi-day visits to the resort within a period of 365 days then an annual pass can be a real bargain. If you go one year in July and the next year in June, for example, then the second year's visits will effectively cost almost nothing.

Blockout dates for the Power Pass:
The Power Pass does not allow you access to the theme parks 365 days a year. These are the dates that are blocked out (i.e. the days you can not enter the parks using the Power Pass):

Universal Studios Florida:
- December 18th – 31st, 2015
- January 1st and 2nd, 2016
- March 19th – April 2nd, 2016
- December 17th – 31st, 2016

Islands of Adventure:
- December 18th – 31st, 2015
- January 1st and 2nd, 2016

- March 19th – April 2nd, 2016
- June 11th – August 15th, 2016
- December 17th – 31st, 2016

All dates are inclusive.

Florida Resident Annual Passes

Florida residents can get discounts on the prices of annual passes. Pricing is as follows: Power Pass - $214.99 plus tax; Preferred Pass - $299.99 plus tax; and Premier Pass - $429.99 plus tax.

Put simply, the features of these passes are exactly the same as the non-Florida resident annual passes mentioned above, except Florida residents pay slightly less for their passes. Proof of residency must be shown when picking up the Florida resident annual pass and/or when entering the turnstiles.

A valid Florida ID must be shown for each annual pass purchased. Accepted IDs are: Florida driver's license; Florida state-issued ID card (must have Florida address); Florida voter's registration card with corresponding photo ID; or College ID from a Florida college or university with corresponding photo ID.

Orlando Flextickets:

The Orlando Flexticket is a ticket option that allows you entry into both Universal Orlando resort theme parks as well as SeaWorld Orlando, Aquatica water park and Wet 'n Wild water park for 14 consecutive days – that is five parks filled with entertainment. It also includes free access to select live entertainment venues at Universal Orlando Resort's CityWalk entertainment complex (visitors must be 21 or older for some venues).

Another benefit of the ticket is that you are only required to pay for parking once each day, regardless of the number of parks visited. You will simply need to show the parking receipt from first park visited that day when visiting the other parks. Pricing for the Orlando Flexticket is $369.95 per adult, and $354.95 per child.

In addition, the Orlando Flexticket Plus option is also available which include access to the five aforementioned parks plus Busch Gardens Tampa Bay for the same period of 14 consecutive days. Pricing for the Orlando Flexticket Plus is $389.95 per adult, and $374.95 per child.

Both these Flexticket options can be purchased online from **www.universalorlando.com** or from a number of ticket brokers.

Chapter 3

Accommodation:

Deciding where you stay whilst on vacation is an important decision: you must consider price, availability, size, location and amenities in order to find the perfect room for you. Luckily, the central Florida area is renowned for having an incredible range of accommodation options to suit all tastes and budgets.

There are numerous nearby hotels that are not located on Universal property which are more reasonably priced than the on-site options. However, we feel that for the full Universal experience you should stay at one of the on-site hotels if you can afford the extra cost. You will be just minutes away from one of the most fun places in Orlando, and some would argue that the benefits of staying on-site more than make up for the extra cost.

In 2015, the Universal Orlando resort went through a process of reclassifying its hotel tiers. There are now three tiers of on-site hotels:
- **Prime Value** – Cabana Bay Beach Resort
- **Preferred** – Royal Pacific Resort, and Sapphire Falls Resort (opens Summer 2016)
- **Premier** – Portofino Bay Hotel, and Hard Rock Hotel

General on-site hotel information:

There are many benefits to staying at on-site Universal Orlando hotels. Read ahead and find out more.

Guests staying at any of the on-site hotels can enjoy the following benefits:
- Early Park Admission to The Wizarding World of Harry Potter one hour before the theme park opens to regular guests.
- Complimentary water taxis, shuttle buses or walking paths to both theme parks and Universal CityWalk.
- Complimentary delivery of merchandise purchased throughout the resort to your hotel.
- Resort-wide charging privileges. Upon leaving your credit card number at check-in, you can use your room key to charge purchases when paying, instead of using your credit or debit card. At the end of your stay you will settle the outstanding balance as one amount.
- Complimentary scheduled transportation to *SeaWorld*, *Aquatica* and *Wet n Wild*. This runs once a day from your hotel *to* these locations and then once or twice a day *from* these parks back to your hotel. The service is called Super Star Shuttle. Seats must be reserved at least 24

hours in advance - this can be done at the concierge desk.

- An option of a wake-up call from one of your favorite Universal Orlando characters.
- Use of the Golf Universal Orlando program.

Additionally, guests staying at Royal Pacific Resort, Portofino Bay Hotel, and Hard Rock Hotel can enjoy the following benefits:

- FREE Universal Express Unlimited ride access to skip the regular lines in both theme parks all day, a benefit that can be worth over $100 per person, per day depending on when you visit.
- Priority seating at select restaurants throughout both theme parks and CityWalk.

Internet Access:
In-room "standard" Wi-Fi access is offered at no cost to hotel guests for the – if you require higher speed access there is a "premium" option available for $15 per day. The lobby and pool areas in all the on-site hotels have free Wi-Fi, which you can access regardless of whether you are staying at the hotel.

Parking:
For all Preferred and Premier hotels parking is charged at $20 per night for self-parking and $27 per night for valet parking (plus tips) – hotel guests pay full price for parking with no discounts.

Day guests who park in the hotel lots will be charged $22 per day, unless they are eating in one of the on-site restaurants where they can have their parking validated for up to 3 hours of complimentary parking.

Parking charges at the Cabana Bay Beach Resort are $12 per night for hotel guests. Day guests will be charged according to their length of stay.

Refrigerators:
Refrigerators are not included in the price of rooms at Royal Pacific Resort, Portofino Bay Hotel, and Hard Rock Hotel. They can be rented for the standard rooms at the price of $15 per night each, plus tax. Those requiring refrigerators for medical conditions may be able to get a discount or the entire cost waived.

Guests staying at Cabana Bay Beach Resort's family suites, and standard rooms at Sapphire Falls Resort have refrigerators included in your nightly room rate.

Character Dining:

The Royal Pacific Resort, Portofino Bay Hotel, and Hard Rock Hotel offer character-dining experiences where you have your food and selected characters visit your table for you to meet, chat with and take photographs.

At Portofino Bay this is at Trattoria del Porto, at Hard Rock Hotel this is at The Kitchen, and at the Royal Pacific Resort you will find this at the Islands Dining Room. Characters vary from Scooby Doo to Shrek and even the Minions from Despicable Me.

Character dining usually takes place once or twice a week between 6:30pm and 9:30pm. Remember you can visit another resort to eat in its restaurant if there is no character dining at your resort during your stay. This applies to non-hotel guests too, as the hotels' dining facilities are open to everyone.

If you drive to an on-site resort hotel for a meal your parking ticket can be validated for up to 3 hours' worth of three parking (except Cabana Bay). Simply ask your server to validate your parking ticket.

Pet rooms:

Pet rooms are available at all Premier and Preferred hotels, although an extra cleaning fee is required of $50 per night, up to a maximum of $150 per room.

Kids Activities:

Kids Activities are available at the three luxury on-site hotels in the evenings for a fee so that the kids can be occupied whilst the parents get to spend some quality time together. Guests from any hotel can use the Kids Activities at other hotels. Information can be obtained from your hotel's concierge desk. Prices usually run about $15 an hour.

Golf Universal Orlando Program:

Although there is no onsite golf course, Universal has created the "Golf Universal Orlando" scheme that allows you to experience two nearby golf clubs – Grand Cypress and Windermere Country – as part of your time at the resort. There is complimentary transportation provided both ways (subject to restrictions). Tee time reservations can be made online at **www.universalorlando.com/golf** or by calling the Royal Pacific Resort, who manage the golf bookings, on (407) 503-3097.

Fitness Suites:

All five on-site hotels have fitness suites. They are complimentary for all guests.

Top Tip: One thing which not widely advertised is that any guest at any on-site hotel can use any of the fitness suites. This means that a guest from Cabana Bay Beach Resort could, for example, visit the gym at the the Hard Rock Hotel with their room key. This is a great benefit that is unheard of elsewhere.

On-site hotel pools:
All the on-site hotels have impressive pools; even more impressively, you can pool hop. Like the fitness suites above, if you are staying at any on-site resort hotel you can use the pool of any resort. A fantastic benefit! Who wouldn't want to try to fun pools at Cabana Bay, the magnificent one at the Hard Rock, and then finish the day with a dip at the new Sapphire Falls pool?

On-site transportation:
When staying at one of the Preferred or Premier level hotels your options to each the theme park include: shuttle buses, water taxis, rickshaws and walking paths. We do not recommend the shuttle buses at these hotels because you won't save time as the drop-off point is the parking garage which is still quite far from the theme parks (about a 10-minute walk).

The water taxis are our preferred form of transportation here, or simply walking. These begin operating from the hotels 30 minutes before Early Park Admission and the last departure from CityWalk is at 2:30am year-round.

The rickshaws are the quickest and most direct way to get around – these are Universal licensed and man-powered and have no set fee, simply tip what you think is appropriate ($2-$4 per person is customary).

For Cabana Bay, the Prime Value resort, you have the option of a walking path or the shuttle buses. The shuttle buses are good but drop you by the parking garage; using the walking paths will take 20 to 25 minutes. The shuttle buses are frequent at all on-site hotels and arrive every 10 to 15 minutes. They are even more frequent at Cabana Bay Beach Resort.

Longer Stays:
Loews, who operates the on-site Universal hotels, offer a promotion called "Stay More, Save More". Savings of up to 35% are available, as can be seen below:

Season	3 Nights	4 Nights	5/6 Nights	7 Nights
Holiday, Peak, and Summer 🔲		10%	15%	25%
Regular and Value 🔲	10%	20%	25%	35%

Cabana Bay Beach Resort:

Hotel Category: Prime Value
Theme: Retro 1950s and '60s
Transport: Walking paths (20 to 25 minutes) or shuttle bus
Number of rooms: 900 standard rooms and 900 family suites
Room size: Standard rooms are 300 square feet and family suites are 430.
Room prices: $124 to $209, plus tax for a standard room. Family suites are priced at $161 to $284, plus tax.
Activities: A 10-lane bowling alley; arcade game room; two resort pools – one with a water slide; s'mores fire pit; hot hub; poolside movies and activities; a store and a fitness center.

We were astounded on our first visit to Cabana Bay Beach Resort. It really does live up to expectations and there is a wealth of activities. You can easily spend several days just exploring all the amenities on offer, and despite the fact this is a large hotel the facilities never felt overcrowded to us.

We like the two sizes of rooms and feel that they are reasonably priced for the location and amenities you get. Standard rooms sleep up to 4 guests, and family suites sleep up to 6.

Even though this resort is significantly cheaper than most of the others, every room still includes a LCD TV, in-room safe, a coffee maker, an iron and a hair-dryer. Suites also include a kitchenette area with a microwave, mini-fridge and sink. We were also particularly appreciative of all the plug sockets in each room, including USB sockets!

The resort does not have a sit down restaurant though you are close enough to visit *CityWalk* or one of the other hotels if you so desire. Instead the resort features a large food court and food trucks outside. In-room pizza delivery is also offered.

Perhaps the biggest surprise is the exceptional entertainment on offer - the 10-lane bowling alley is unheard of elsewhere ($15 per game, shoe rental $4 per pair, and food is available), and many other amenities that are more commonly found in higher-priced resorts are available here too.

There are two pools at the resort. The main pool at 10,000 square feet has a water slide, and the smaller 8000 square foot pool has as a sandy beach. Both pools offer accessible zero-entry access. The smaller pool even has a lazy river going around it spanning 700 feet. Free poolside activities happen throughout the day.

Self-service laundry is available for $3 per wash and $3 per dryer load. Parking is charged at $12 per night for self-parking, payable at check-in.

There are, however, a few downsides to this resort: guests staying at Cabana Bay will NOT receive complimentary Express Passes - this is usually cited as one of the main reasons for staying on-site. Guests will also not be able to reach the hotel via water taxis and must use buses instead or be prepared to walk up to 25 minutes from their room to the theme parks and *CityWalk*.

Cabana Bay is currently being expanded with two new towers housing 400 additional guest rooms – these will open in 2017. While this is good news for those looking to stay at the resort, we hope the additional guests will not put strain on the current facilities.

Dining:
Bayline Diner – Quick service food court. Entrees priced at $7 to $8.50 for breakfast, and $6 to $12.50 for lunch and dinner.
Galaxy Bowl Restaurant – Table service dining and quick-service food available too. Open from 11:00am to 10:00pm. Entrees priced at $6 to $10.
Atomic Tonic – Poolside bar with drinks and limited snacks. Cocktails $9 to $13.
The Hideaway Bar & Grill – Poolside Bar and grilled fare
Swizzle Lounge – Bar. Cocktails priced at $9 to $11. Other drinks from $6.
Starbucks – Quick service location.

Loews Sapphire Falls Resort: (Opens July 14th, 2016)

Hotel Category: Preferred
Theme: Caribbean-inspired
Transport: Water taxis, pedicabs, walking paths (15 to 20 minutes) and shuttle buses.
Number of rooms: 1000 rooms including 83 suites
Room size: Standard rooms are 364 square feet, and suites start at 529 square feet.
Room prices: $179 to $259, plus tax for a standard room
Activities: A large pool, two white sand beaches, a hot tub, children's water play area with pop-up jets, and a water slide; fire pit for s'mores; complimentary fitness center for guests including a dry sauna; arcade game room; and a Universal Store.

The newest resort to the Universal Orlando on-site hotel series of properties promises to be beautiful, tropical and relaxing destination. The theming and level of immersion at this hotel hugely exciting.

The centerpiece to this resort is the 16,000 square foot pool, the largest in Orlando, as well as the two sandy beaches, and water slide for added fun. Cabana rentals are also available around the pool.

Standard queen rooms sleep up to five people – the fifth person will need a roll-away bed at a supplement of $25 per night.

There is also a 115,000 square foot convention space for any business travelers. Although the hotel does not open until Summer 2016, reservations are already open.

Note: This hotel does not have complimentary unlimited Express Pass for the theme parks, and guests will not receive priority seating at select restaurants. Both these perks are reserved for the more expensive hotels which follow.

Dining:

New Dutch Trading Co. – New Dutch Trading Co. is the grab-and-go option for families who want to stock up before heading off on adventures. With ready to go meals, beverages, fresh-baked breads and homemade jams, this is the stop for provisions and supplies.

Strong Water Tavern – A wall of vintage rums, your own rum specialist, a ceviche bar and a patio overlooking the lagoon combine to make Strong Water Tavern a very unique watering hole. Serving lunch and dinner, with daily rum tastings, this lounge is a true destination.

Amatista Cookhouse – Caribbean cuisine prepared in an exhibition kitchen makes Amatista Cookhouse an instantly inviting option for breakfast, lunch or dinner. Whether dining indoors or out—or in one of the private dining areas—guests of Amatista Cookhouse will feel welcomed and relaxed in this vibrant and inspiring restaurant.

Drhum Club Kantine – Nestled within the lush grounds of the pool, Drhum Club Kantine offers sun-seekers a delightful Tapas-style menu focusing on fresh seafood and taste-tempting tropical drinks. The adjoining fire-pit area, awash in the rhythms of the islands, is the perfect spot to indulge in an afternoon or evening libation.

Sapphire Falls also has 24-hour room service available.

Loews Royal Pacific Resort:

Hotel Category: Preferred
Theme: Tropical Paradise
Transport: Water taxis, pedicabs, walking paths (15 to 20 minutes) and shuttle buses.
Number of rooms: 1000
Room size: 335 square feet in a standard room
Room prices: $244 to $419 per night, plus tax
Activities: One very large pool, volleyball court, kids' water play area, fitness center, croquet, poolside activities, a torch lighting ceremony, and the Wantilan Luau dinner show.

The Royal Pacific Resort is stunningly well-themed. From the moment you step inside you are in a different world: a world away from the hustle and bustle of Orlando's theme parks. Yet, they are conveniently located just next door for easy access.

There may only be one pool at this hotel, but (until Sapphire Fall opens in the summer) it is the largest in the city of Orlando. Use of the volleyball court is complimentary and a ball can be obtained from the pool towel location. "Dive-In movies" are screened by the pool on select nights. Cabanas with a TV, complimentary bottled water and sodas, a ceiling fan and fruit are priced starting at $100 per day. Cabana rentals can be made in person at The Gymnasium or by calling (407) 503-3235.

The Gymnasium features a variety of cardio machines and free weight equipment, and is complimentary for guests. There are also steam and sauna facilities in each locker room, and a co-ed whirlpool. Use of these is also complimentary.

On Friday and Saturday nights (and Tuesdays during the peak summer season) guests can enjoy the 'Torch Lighting Ceremony' with hula dancers and fire jugglers by the pool – there is no charge to watch this event.

An on-site coin-operated laundry is available. Prices are $3 per wash, and $3 per dryer load.

Dining:
Orchid Court Lounge and Sushi Bar – Continental breakfast, and sushi bar. Breakfast entrees priced at $9 to $10. Bar entrees priced at $12 to $20.
Islands Dining Room – Table service dining. Breakfast buffet or a la Carte available, buffet priced at $19.50 per adult and $10 per child. All day menu entrees priced at $16 to $30.
Jake's American Bar – Bar, with light snacks and larger meals. Entrees priced at $10 to $30.
Bula Bar and Grille – Poolside bar and dining. Entrees priced at $11 to $15.
Emeril's Tchoup Chop – Signature table service dining. Entrees priced at $12 to $18 at lunch, and $24 to $30 at dinner.
Wantilan Luau – Hawaiian dinner show starting at 5:00pm or 6:00pm on Saturdays (and Tuesdays during peak season). Reservations required. Features a buffet including non-alcoholic and select alcoholic drinks. Buffet priced at $63 to $70 for adults, and $35 to $40 for children.

Dining Top Tip: Try Tchoup Chop's outside bar which serves the full menu from inside as well as cocktails. It can be a quick way to get a seat when the restaurant is busy.

Top Tip 1: If you choose to walk from this hotel to CityWalk, the distance covered will be about 1/3 of a mile.

Top Tip 2: Because of the location of the ferry terminals and its proximity to *Universal's Islands of Adventure* it is generally quicker to walk from this resort to *Islands of Adventure* than use the water taxi service. The same applies for the *CityWalk* area. The water taxi is more relaxing, though.

Hard Rock Hotel Orlando:

Hotel Category: Premier
Theme: Rock 'n' Roll
Transport: Water taxis, pedicabs, walking paths (5 minutes to Universal Studios Florida and 10 minutes to Islands of Adventure) and shuttle buses.
Number of rooms: 650 rooms, including 33 suites
Room size: 375 square feet for a standard room
Room prices: $278 to $479 per night, plus tax
Activities: Pool, Jacuzzis, poolside movies, volleyball court, and a fitness center

You will feel like rock 'n' roll royalty with impeccable accommodation, a wealth of recreation, and personal service and attention fit for an "A-List" celebrity at The Hard Rock Hotel – the place is lively, yet laid back. Rock fans will love the location where there is over $1 million of music-related memorabilia. Classy, yet totally casual, this is a true deluxe hotel.

The highlight of the hotel is the huge 12,000 square feet pool which features zero entry leveling and white sand. It even has an underwater sound system and a slide! The area also has a beach with a volleyball court and lounge chairs. There are two Jacuzzis, including one that is designated for adults only. Poolside orders from the bar are available. Most nights there is a "dive-in movie" by the pool, and there are occasionally dive-in concerts too.

Cabanas can be rented from $80 to $200 per day, depending on the location of the cabana and the season. Cabanas include soft drinks and bottled water, a TV, fresh fruit, towels and a refrigerator.

One unique feature of this resort hotel is all the extra musical fun you can have – for example, DJ lessons are held daily during peak seasons in the lobby. What's more if you are a guitar fan then you will love the fact that you can rent out a Fender by AXE guitar at no extra cost during your stay, though a $1000 deposit is required.

Laundry is priced at $3 per wash and $3 per dryer load.

This hotel is the closest to CityWalk and the theme parks, being located right next door to *Universal Studios Florida* – a brilliant location that is only a few minutes walk to theme park fun.

Top Tip: Look for the plaques next to the musical memorabilia throughout the hotel; each of these has a unique number on it. Call (407) 503-2233 and enter the number on the plaque to learn more about the item you are looking at.

Dining:
The Palm Restaurant – Table service dining, steak house. Entrees priced at $12 to $60.
Velvet Bar – Bar with light snacks and bigger plates too. Entrees priced at $12 to $36.
The Kitchen – Buffet at breakfast. Table Service dining at lunch and dinner. Entrees priced at $11 to $37.
Emack & Bolio's – Ice creams, pizzas and small bites. Entrees priced at $9 to $23.
BeachClub – Bar and quick service snacks.

Reservations for table serving dining establishments can be made at OpenTable.com

Velvet Sessions – The Ultimate Cocktail Party
From January to October, on the last Thursday of each month you can experience Velvet Sessions. The event is described as "a rock & roll cocktail party held in the hotel's Velvet Bar and Lobby Lounge. Each "Session" showcases a different type of beverage theme for members to sip, shoot or guzzle along with fabulous and great live music from the nation's best rock bands."

Tickets are $29 in advance from **www.velvetsessions.com** or $35 at the door. VIP tickets are $50. Each ticket includes: Complimentary specialty drinks, finger foods and warm-up tunes, starting at 6:30pm until show time at 8:30pm. During the show and afterwards, there is a cash bar. After the band performs, stick around for a DJ set until 1:00am. This event is for ages 21 and over only. Past performers include: Brett Michaels, Joan Jett, The Tubes, Blue Oyster Cult, ABC and Foreigner to name but a few.

Loews Portofino Bay Hotel:

Hotel Category: Premier
Theme: The seaside village of Portofino, Italy
Transport: Water taxis, pedicabs, walking paths (about 20 minutes) and shuttle buses.
Number of rooms: 750 rooms, including 39 suites
Room size: 450 square feet for a standard room
Room prices: $304 to $494 per night, plus tax
Activities: 3 pools, poolside movies, spa (paid), live music.

This premier hotel recreates the charm and romance of the famed seaside village of Portofino, Italy, right down to the cobblestone streets and outdoor cafes.

This is the most luxurious of the onsite hotels and the theming is truly mind-blowing. However, families who want a fun addition to their room, may want to consider one of the 18 Despicable Me themed Kids Suites with a separate bedroom for the kids.

The hotel has 3 pools. The Beach Pool has a waterslide and is the largest and grandest of the pools. The Villa Pool also has a Jacuzzi-style area. The Hillside Pool is the quietest and the most relaxing, with a view along the Bay. On Saturdays during peak seasons there is a "Dive-In Movie" for guests to enjoy.

Pool cabanas are available for hire at the Beach Pool and the Villa Pool for those wanting to live the real luxurious lifestyle – these include overhead fans, a TV, and a mini refrigerator stocked with water and soft drinks, and complimentary fruit. Prices start at $75 per day. Reservations can be made in person at the Beach Pool hut or by calling (407) 503-1200 or 41745 from the in-room phone.

The Mandara Spa, a brand synonymous with luxury treatments, is located by the beach and offers a variety of indulgent experiences. The most basic 50-minute Swedish massage starts at $130, and you can expect to pay up to $595 for the "Nirvana…Bliss for a Day" experience that lasts over 6 hours. Facials, body therapies, nail services, waxing and haircuts are also available. Taxes and a 20% service charge also apply. Any treatment purchased also includes full use of the spa and fitness facilities. A fitness day pass can also be purchased for $25 for non-hotel guests. Spa treatment reservations can be made by calling 407-503-1244.

There is no coin operated guest laundry at this hotel. You can either use the hotel's laundry service or take your clothes to Hard Rock Hotel a few minutes away and wash them there.

We would advise taking the water taxi from this hotel to the theme parks. The walking path is lovely but it is a 20-minute walk.

In the evenings, weather permitting, the Portofino Bay Hotel piazza has live music and classical singers, and guests can enjoy the Italian atmosphere.

One unique location at this resort is Family Art Photography where you can have a complimentary family photo-shoot at no charge. This can be done as a classic family portrait, poolside or even underwater. Sessions last 15 to 30 minutes. The session is at no charge, but the photo prints themselves are the standard prices charged everywhere for this type of work. Items vary from prints to canvases and even tiles. One 8"x10" print costs about $30, and four 6x6 metallic gloss finish prints will set you back $184, for example. Two 11"x14" canvases cost $194. A DVD of your entire shoot will set you back $375. Prices exclude tax. There is the option of ordering when you return home online at http://www.familyartonline.com.

Dining:
Bice – Table service gourmet dining. Entrees priced at $19 to $48.
The Thirsty Fish Bar – Bar with light snacks. Open from 6:00pm onwards.
Trattoria del Porto – Table service dining. Entrees priced at $9 to $18 at breakfast, and $9 and up for lunch and dinner.
Mama Della's Ristorante – Family style dining
Sal's Market Deli – Quick service dining. Serves sandwiches, paninis and pizzas.
Gelateria Caffe Espresso – Coffees and ice creams priced at $3 to $7.
Bar American – Upscale bar, also serves food. Open from 4:00pm to 11:00pm. Entrees $15 to $16. Small bites $10 to $14.
Splendido Pizzeria – Pizza, salads and sandwiches served poolside. Entrees priced at $13 to $18.

Reservations for table service dining establishments can be made at opentable.com.

Harbor Nights:
Four times per year, the Portofino Bay resort hosts 'Harbor Nights', a wine tasting and jazz event designed to capture the ambiance of the Mediterranean. Each event features select wines, gourmet food, live music and other live entertainment. Pricing is usually $45 per person in advance, or $55 on the door (subject to availability). A VIP seating option is priced at $75. All prices exclude tax. There is even a Holiday edition with a tree-lighting ceremony.

Chapter 4

Getting there:

Before we get too carried away with all the fun you can have at the Universal Orlando Resort, you must first make your way there. Here are some of your options:

By car:

Universal Orlando Resort is located about 10 miles southwest of the city of Orlando, Florida and about 10 miles northeast of the Walt Disney World Resort. Universal Orlando can be reached easily by car from the Interstate 4 (I-4) and then following Universal Blvd north to the parking garages. For your GPS, the address you want is *6000 Universal Blvd, Orlando, FL.*

The parking garages are very big and can accommodate about 20,000 vehicles so be sure to remember where you parked. Garages open at least 90 minutes before official park opening time and all levels except the roof level are covered which means you will not come back to a car that has been in the sun all day or have to walk through the rain to get to your vehicle.

Top Tip: When approaching the parking toll plaza where you pay, stay in the leftmost lane – everyone else stays to the right for some reason and you can shave off 5 to 10 minutes to waiting time this way on busy days.

There is an easy to remember parking system - each parking spot is assigned a character name and a number - make sure to note it   down as it could save you hours later on! A good tip is to take a photo of your parking location (but also write it down in case your phone or camera battery dies). The garages are located approximately 5 to 10 minutes walk away from the theme parks.

Parking is $20 per day for self-parking (free for Preferred and Premium Annual Passholders). This last increased in October 2015. Preferred parking is $25 (discounted for Preferred Annual Passholders and free for Premier Passholders) and valet parking is $35 a day ($15 for Preferred Annual Passholders and free for Premier Passholders). "Red carpet valet" parking is available for a $10 surcharge that guarantees you will get your car within 5 minutes.

Disabled parking bays are available; just make sure to request them. These are located slightly closer to CityWalk and the theme parks.

Lunchtime visitors to *CityWalk* can get free valet parking by validating their restaurant receipt from Monday to Friday for two hours of free parking. Contact your restaurant for the specific hours of this offer. A signposted passenger drop-off point is also available.

Between 6:00pm and 10:00pm parking is $5 for visitors, and is free for Florida residents with proof of residency. After 10:00pm parking is free for all guests – a good reason to visit *CityWalk* in the evening. However, for busy evenings like Halloween Horror Nights expect parking to be full price throughout the entire day.

After parking you will walk to the main parking rotunda hub, go through bag check and then walk through CityWalk – at the end of CityWalk you can turn left for *Universal's Islands of Adventure* or right for *Universal Studios Florida.*

Walt Disney World Resort to Universal Orlando Resort by car:
This is a common route as many visitors to Universal Orlando start off their vacation at the Walt Disney World Resort. You will first need to follow internal resort signs to the Interstate 4 (I-4). There are entrances to the I-4 by ESPN: Wide World of Sports, Disney's Pop Century Resort, Disney's Typhoon Lagoon water park, and Disney Springs.

Follow the I-4 North/East for 6 to 8 miles depending on where you got on, take exit 75A and merge onto Universal Blvd, the address you want is "6000 Universal Blvd, Orlando" but at this point you will be able to follow local road signs to the parking garages.

Public Transport:
There are two options for those using public transport - the I-Ride Trolley and the Lynx buses. The I-Ride follows a route along International Drive and is aimed at tourists, whereas Lynx buses are used frequently by locals and are often busier at peak times.

Both services have a stop just outside Wet 'n' Wild water park which is where you should get off (on the I-Ride this is stop 8). From there it is a 15 to 20-minute walk to the Universal parking plaza area. Cross the road and head north on Universal Blvd towards the theme parks until you reach the overhead walkway, which you will use to enter Universal Orlando.

Both options are fairly inexpensive at about $2 each – take a look at both options online and decide on which is best for you.

Note: Be careful! You do have to cross a few major roads and one smaller road (which does not have traffic lights) on the short walk from the bus stops to the Universal Orlando resort.

Top Tip: Orlando public transport can be very infrequent with sometimes only 1 or 2 buses an hour so be sure to check the schedule in advance.

Walt Disney World to Universal Orlando Resort by public transport:
This is a common route as many visitors to Universal Orlando start off their vacation at the Walt Disney World Resort. Go to the Transportation and Ticket Center (TTC) on Walt Disney World resort property; for most guests this will involve going to Magic Kingdom Park and then taking the monorail over to the TTC. At the TTC ask a Cast Member for the location of the LYNX bus stop. Alternatively, you can catch the Lynx bus at Disney Springs– we recommend you use Google Maps to locate this top. At either the TTC or Disney Springs, you will catch the number 50 LYNX bus.

Be sure to have exact change for the bus as there is no change from the fare machine – the machine accepts coins and dollar bills. Ask the bus driver for a transfer (valid for 90 minutes from first issue) as you will be using more than one bus and this way you will only need to pay once. The price is $2 per person.

Once you are on the number 50 bus you will be on it for approximately 35 minutes until you reach the first stop on Sea Harbor Drive. The exact location of the stop you will want to get off at is *6800 Sea Harbor Dr and Central Florida Pky.*

Here you will need to wait for the number 8 LYNX bus and stay on that bus until *6200 International Dr and Universal Blvd.* Be sure to ask the driver for the Universal stop if you are unsure. This number 8 bus journey will take about 15 minutes.

From here you will walk to the Universal Orlando Resort – this is about a 15 to 20-minute walk. The total journey time with transfers is about 1 hour 15 minutes to 1 hour 30 minutes each way.

Take a look at **http://www.golynx.com/** for help with the LYNX bus service, including instructional videos and maps.

Shuttle services:
Unlike guests staying at Walt Disney World's on-site hotels, there is no complimentary shuttle or motor coach transportation between the Universal Orlando Resort and Orlando International Airport.

Many companies provide a shuttle service. We have found Mears Transportation and Super Shuttle to be reliable, though many other services are available. Prices are roughly $30 to $35 per person return, or about $20 one-way.

Walt Disney World to Universal Orlando by shuttle:
A Super Shuttle charter quote for this route is about $45 for a 4-seater vehicle for a one-way trip, excluding tip. A taxi will work out cheaper. See below.

Taxis:

This is the option we recommend if you coming to the Universal Orlando Resort from the airport and do not drive, especially if there are several of you. The cost should not usually be more than about $55-70 including a tip each way. Mears Transportation offers a taxi service and we have found this company to be reliable, though many other services are available.

Walt Disney World to Universal Orlando by taxi:
Taxi prices vary but a quote (from Mears for example) will usually be about $35 for a taxi from EPCOT to Universal Orlando, excluding tip. UberX quotes vary from $20 to $35.

Chapter 5

Universal Studios Florida - Park Guide

Universal Studios Florida opened in 1990 as the Floridian cousin to the popular Universal Studios theme park in Hollywood. The original idea of the park was to experience how movies are made. Actual filming would be done in the park too. Over the years the focus of the park has changed slightly and the philosophy is now to ride and "experience the movies" for yourself, rather than seeing how they are made. The park hosted 8.2 million guests in 2014.

Note: Average attraction waits noted in this section here are estimates for busy summer days when on school break. Wait times may well be lower at other times of the year. They may also occasionally be higher, especially during the week of 4th July, Thanksgiving, Christmas, New Year and other public holidays.

When we list restaurant food prices, this information was accurate during our last visit to the restaurant. We also do not post the full menu but just a sample of the food on offer. Meal prices stated in this section do not include a drink unless otherwise stated. When an attraction is listed as requiring lockers, all loose items must be stored in complimentary lockers outside each attraction.

Production Central

Production Central is the gateway to Universal Studios Florida - you must pass through it to get to the rest of the park and you will walk through it again when exiting. Here you will find **Despicable Me: Minion Mayhem, Hollywood Rip Ride Rockit, Shrek 4D** and **TRANSFORMERS: The Ride-3D**.

Production Central is also where **Guest Services** is located where you can get help with disability assistance, dining reservations, questions, compliments and complaints. You can also exchange some currencies at this location. Guest Services is located to the right-hand side after the turnstiles. To the left of the turnstiles you will find lockers, as well as stroller and wheelchair rentals.

The **Studio Audience Center** (to the right after the turnstiles) is the place to get tickets for any shows being filmed in the soundstages at the Universal Orlando Resort. Tickets are complimentary. This is also the location for Lost and Found.

First Aid is located next to the Studio Audience Center. Another First Aid station is located next to Louie's Italian Restaurant.

You will also find the **American Express Passholder Lounge** in this area of the park, opposite the Shrek attraction shop. This lounge is reserved for those who use an AmEx card to buy park tickets or an annual pass. Inside the lounge you will find bottled water, snacks and phone charging facilities. Simply show your ticket receipt and ticket itself, as well as your AmEx card for entry. Guests who simply use an AmEx card for in-park purchases but have not used it to purchase their entry tickets into the park do not have access to this lounge.

If you need to **mail** something, you can drop off your letters and postcards at the mailbox, located to the left as you come in after the turnstiles, to the right of the lockers. Stamps can be bought from the *On Location* shop here on the Front Lot. **Calling cards** can be bought from a vending machine near the lockers.

Family & Health Services, which includes a nursing room, is located to the right after the turnstiles.

Despicable Me: Minion Mayhem

Height Restriction: 40 inches (1.02m)
Attraction length: 4 minutes + 2 pre-shows totaling 12 minutes
Express Pass Available: Yes
Average Wait: 60 to 120 minutes
Lockers required: No
A simulator based ride with several individual simulator vehicles in front of one screen featuring 4D effects. 'Despicable Me' fans will come out very excited but others may miss some of the cuteness. Due to the low hourly capacity and the immense popularity of its characters, queues are almost always lengthy for this attraction.

Top Tip: A stationary version of this attraction is also offered where you sit in benches at the front of the theatre room. These do not move, but you still get the same 3D experience. When this is offered the wait time is usually very short, e.g. 10 minutes instead of 90 minutes. There is a separate queue line for this.

Fun fact: The trees planted outside the ride are banana trees, as the minions love the yellow fruit so much!

Hollywood Rip Ride Rockit

Height Restriction: Minimum 51 inches (1.29m) / Maximum 79 inches (2.00m)
Capacity: 1850 people per hour
Attraction length: 1 minute 45 seconds
Express Pass Available: Yes
Average Wait: 45 to 90 minutes
Lockers required: Yes
One of the newer experiences in the park, this coaster truly dominates the skyline of the park. Once you board the vehicle, get ready to be held in by just a lap bar-style restraint. On this ride you get to choose a song on a touchscreen to play. This will pump into your ears through individual seat speakers as your adrenaline races. Think of this as a bit like *Rock 'n' Rollercoaster* at Disney but with more music choices, without the loops and a big initial drop. The initial 'almost-a-loop' is really fun, as you go a loop but stay upright all the way round - a really unique experience. Once you are done, you can even purchase an on-ride music video of your entire experience! A single rider line is available at this attraction.

Top Tip: Don't trust the single rider wait time that is posted at the entrance to the attraction. We have often waited less than half of the official posted single rider wait. The wait time from the bottom of the stairs to being on the train is usually approximately 30 minutes so walk in to the line and determine the time yourself from that.

Top Tip 2: As well as the songs displayed on the screen, there are many secret bonus songs. To access the, after lowering your restraint you will need to push and hold the ride logo on the screen for about 10 seconds and then type in a three-digit number. A full list of the songs is available online with a quick search.

Top Tip 3: The Pocket RockIt Rollercoaster Setlist iPhone app, available on the Apple App Store, lists the full song list including hidden songs. The app costs $0.99.

Shrek 4-D

Height Restriction: None. No handheld infants.
Capacity: 2500-3000 people per hour
Attraction length: 12 minutes for the main show + 5 minutes pre-show
Express Pass Available: Yes
Average Wait: 15 to 45 minutes
Lockers required: No
Stepping into Shrek 4D, you know you are getting into a different kind of attraction – even Universal says that is not just a 3D, but a 4D experience. The unique part of this attraction is the seats, which are able to create incredible sensations, acting like personal simulators. For those not wishing to experience the seat movement, a limited number of stationary seats are also available. The film itself is interesting and is great fun with some corny jokes and jabs at Disney thrown in for good measure.

TRANSFORMERS: The Ride-3D

Height Restriction: 40 inches (1.02m)
Capacity: Approximately 1800 people per hour
Attraction length: 4 minutes 30 seconds
Express Pass Available: Yes
Average Wait: 90 to 150 minutes.
Lockers required: No

TRANSFORMERS is a 3D screen-based moving ride, similar to *The Amazing Adventures of Spiderman* in *Universal's Islands of Adventure*. For those who have never watched Transformers, the storyline follows Autobots trying to get the Allspark. The ride is an enjoyable experience but in our opinion it just does not live up to how good *Spiderman* is - considering *Spiderman* is over 15 years old, it feels like almost no technological or storytelling progress has been made since then. This ride will often have the longest queue in the park, after the rides in *The Wizarding World of Harry Potter: Diagon Alley*. A single rider line is available.

Fun fact: Ever wondered how such a long ride is packed into such a small building? Engineers came up with an ingenious way to reduce the ride's overall footprint: during the ride whilst you are watching a scene on one of the giant screens you are actually taken in an elevator up one floor which houses another level of ride track. Here the ride continues its course and towards the end of the ride you come back down to the first floor via another elevator whilst you watch another giant screen – this is all done seamlessly and really is an incredible feat.

Restaurants:

Universal Studios' Classic Monster Cafe – Quick Service. Accepts Universal Dining Plan. Serves chicken, lasagna, cheeseburgers, pizza and more. Entrees are priced at $7.50 to $11.50.

New York:

This area of the park is themed around the big apple. Attractions in this area of the park include **Revenge of the Mummy** and the **Blues Brothers Show**. This was formerly the area of an attraction called TWISTER, but that has now closed and is due to be replaced by a Jimmy Fallon attraction in 2017.

Revenge of the Mummy

Height Restriction: 48 inches (1.22m)
Capacity: 2000 people per hour
Attraction length: 4 minutes
Express Pass Available: Yes
Average Wait: 20 to 60 minutes
Lockers required: Yes

An incredibly unique rollercoaster featuring fire, smoke, forward motion, backwards motion, turns and much more. The whole ride is fantastic and is one of the most fun coaster we have been on, starting off as a dark ride and developing into a coaster. Although the ride does not go upside down and is not exactly the fastest attraction in Orlando, it does tell its story very well and really immerses you in the atmosphere. It is a great thrill with plot twists throughout. A single rider line is available.

The queue line is also really detailed and contains several interactive elements. For example, there is a scarab beetle that you can press whilst watching other guests via a screen. If you press the beetle, the guests will feel a quick blast of air from underneath them, guaranteed to give them a fright. But beware where you put your hands in line, as the treasure you see around you may not be all you think it is and you might just be in for a surprise or two.

Fun fact: The Mummy ride replaced *Kongfrontation* (a ride based on King Kong), which was once housed in the same building; a statue of the great ape has been left behind as a tribute in the treasure room.

The Blues Brothers Show

Get ready to see Jake and Elwood, the Blues Brothers themselves, take to the stage in this show. Unlike other shows where you have to arrive in good time and sit in a show-style amphitheater, the Blues Brothers Show is simply on a small stage in a street with more of a street-performer feel to it. Crowds are not very big and most people just walk in and out during the show. To be honest, this is not one of our favorite shows.

Rock Climbing

Located near The Revenge of the Mummy attraction, there is a small alleyway which offers a 50-foot tall rockclimbing wall. Once you reach the top, ring the bell and be victorious!

Restaurants:

Finnegan's Bar and Grill – Table Service location. Accepts Universal Dining Plan. Serves salads, sandwiches, fish and chips, chicken, corned beef, sirloin steak and more. Entrees are priced at $10 to $22. This is our favorite place to eat in this park outside of Diagon Alley.

Louie's Italian Restaurant – Quick Service location. Accepts Universal Dining Plan. Serves spaghetti and meatballs, pizza slices, whole pizza pies and fettuccine alfredo. Entrees are priced at $6 to $14. Whole pizza pies are priced between $29 and $36.

San Francisco

This area of the park has changed immensely over the years, especially due to the closure of the Jaws ride to make way for The Wizarding World of Harry Potter: Diagon Alley a few years ago. Now, San Francisco is once again going through a major redevelopment. "Disaster!" closed in September 2015. Beetlejuice's Graveyard Revue also held its last performance on December 2nd, 2015. This area will be redeveloped to make way for a brand new ride – Fast & Furious: Supercharged – which will open in 2017.

Restaurants:

Richter's Burger Co. – Quick Service location. Accepts Universal Dining Plan. Serves cheeseburgers, salads, and chicken sandwiches. Entrees are priced at $8 to $10.50.

Lombard's Seafood Grille – Table Service location. Accepts Universal Dining Plan. Serves salads, sandwiches, catch of the day, sirloin steak, stir-fry and more. Entrees are priced at $9 to $20.

San Francisco Pastry Company – Sandwiches and Pastries location. Accepts Universal Dining Plan. Entrees are priced at $3 to $9.50.

World Expo

World Expo is home to both a **MEN IN BLACK** attraction, as well as a **Simpsons** area. You will also find **Fear Factor: LIVE** as the area's live show.

MEN IN BLACK: Alien Attack

Height Restriction: 42 inches (1.07m)
Capacity: 2200 people per hour
Attraction length: 5 minutes
Express Pass Available: Yes
Average Wait: Less than 45 minutes
Lockers required: Yes

At Men In Black it is your job to protect the city and defeat the aliens. You are dispatched in teams and compete against another team of riders. This ride is a fun, family-friendly, immersive experience that we highly recommend. A single rider line is available.

Top Tip: Keep holding down the trigger throughout the ride. You get points for doing this regardless of whether you hit any targets or not. For major points you will need to find and shoot Frank the Pug who is hidden in the ride. You will find Frank in the newspaper stand on the right hand side of the second room.

The Simpsons Ride

Height Restriction: 40 inches (1.02m)
Capacity: 1600 people per hour
Attraction length: 6 minutes
Express Pass Available: Yes
Average Wait: 20 to 40 minutes
Lockers required: No

How about riding a simulated rollercoaster? The Simpsons characters have you covered. This is a fun filled simulator in front of an enormous screen. Your adventure is filled with gags throughout and overall is a fun family experience. Simpsons fans will be in love!

Fun fact: During the pre-show video keep an eye out for the DeLorean car and Doc Brown from Back to the Future. This is a tribute to the 'Back to the Future' attraction that used to be in the same building.

Fear Factor Live

Capacity: 1800 people per show
Show length: 20 minutes
Express Pass Available: Yes
Lockers required: No

Get ready to watch real theme park guests face their fears live on stage as they compete against each other in Fear Factor Live. Or alternatively, why not apply and be one of those guests? If you would like to participate in the show you will want to be near the entrance 60 to 90 minutes before the next show is scheduled to start. Guests must be over 18, have photo ID on them and be in good physical condition to participate. Volunteers are also chosen to play minor roles during the show.

This show is starting to show its age, in our opinion, and we expect it to be replaced in the coming years but for the moment it's a fun amusement.

Restaurants:

Fast Food Boulevard – Quick Service location. Accepts Universal Dining Plan. From the outside this location appears to be several separate Simpson's-themed buildings. Inside, you will find one big ordering area. You will find:

- **Moe's Tavern** sells Buzz Cola, Flaming Moes and Duff Beer (priced $3 to $8)
- **Lisa's Teahouse of Horror** sells salads and wraps (priced $6 to $10)
- **Luigi's** which sells personal-sized pizzas (priced $7 to $8)
- **The Frying Dutchman** sells fish (priced $4 to $14)
- **Cletus' Chicken Shack** sells fried chicken and chicken sandwiches (priced $8 to $11)
- **Krusty Burger** sells burgers and hot dogs ($8 to $13),

Hollywood:

The Hollywood area of the park has no rides but does house the park's two best shows: **Universal's Horror Make Up Show** and **Terminator 2: 3-D**.

Universal's Horror Make Up Show

Show length: Approximately 25 minutes
Express Pass Available: Yes
Lockers required: No

A fun show that is sure to have you in stitches. Go behind the scenes and see how gory and scary effects are accomplished in films. The show's script is very well thought out with laugh after laugh, and there is some fun audience interaction too. This is one show we highly recommend you visit! The theatre is relatively small so make sure to arrive early.

If you want to be selected to be part of the show, the actors tend to go for young women located in the middle section of the theatre. They also tend to go for someone who they think will speak little or no English, for comedic effect.

Note: The show has set performance times and usually runs about every 45 minutes.

Terminator 2: 3-D

Show length: About 25 minutes including the main show (12 minutes) and the pre-show
Express Pass Available: Yes
Average Wait: Less than 15 minutes
Capacity: 2500 to 2800 people per hour
Terminator 2: 3-D is an incredible mix of live-action, 3D and in-theatre special effects. This show is unlike any theme park show we have ever seen and is hugely enjoyable. The 3D is incredibly well accomplished and merges seamlessly with the live actors, meaning sometimes it is difficult to figure out what is on screen and what is actually in front of you.

A warning for those easily startled that there are some loud pyrotechnic bangs throughout the show and there are sudden jolts in the seats. There are stationary seats available. If you do not enjoy loud shows, then Terminator 2 is most definitely not for you but it would be a shame to miss out on such an incredible show. The show runs at set times: usually about every 20 to 45 minutes.

Top Tip: There is usually no need to turn up more than 5 minutes before the posted time, as there are plenty of seats in the theatre for each show.

Restaurants:

Mel's Drive In – Quick Service location. Serves cheeseburgers and root beer floats. Accepts Universal Dining Plan. Entrees are priced at $8 to $10.50.
Beverly Hills Boulangerie – Quick Service location. Accepts Universal Dining Plan. Serves sandwiches, pastries, cakes, soups and salads. Entrees are priced at $7 to $12.

Woody Woodpecker's Kid Zone

This is the area of the park dedicated to the smaller members of the family. Universal isn't just for adrenaline junkies as is proven here. Live shows include **Animal Actors on Location** and **A Day in the Park with Barney**. **Woody Woodpecker's Nuthouse Coaster** and **E.T. Adventure** are both rides, but they do both have a minimum height limit. **Fievel's Playland** and **Curious George Goes to Town** are two large play areas where kids can spend hours playing.

Animal Actors on Location

Show length: 20 minutes
Express Pass Available: Yes
Lockers required: No
A behind the scenes look at how animals are taught to act in films – there is even some audience participation. In our opinion, the show is lackluster with a big reliance on video clips and a lack of flow. It is a shame to see this show, especially when compared to a similar show at Disney's Animal Kingdom that only features birds – Disney's show has humor, a great storyline and a real wow factor. This one just doesn't. We would advise you to give this a miss unless you are a big animal fan.

A Day in the Park with Barney

Show length: 15 minutes
Express Pass Available: Yes
Lockers required: No
Come and join Barney and his friends for a fun-filled show where little ones can even sing along. After the show is over there is a play area to explore, and you can usually meet and greet Barney too.

Curious George Goes to Town

A play area filled with water. Be sure to bring a change of clothes for the little ones.

Top Tip: If you want to walk through the area and go to the factory without getting wet, simply follow the signposted "dry path".

Woody Woodpecker's Nuthouse Coaster

Height Restriction: 36 inches (0.92m)
Capacity: 780 people per hour
Attraction length: 44 seconds
Express Pass Available: Yes
Average Wait: 30 minutes or less
Lockers required: No

Think of *Woody Woodpecker's Nuthouse Coaster* as a kid's first coaster – a way to get them introduced into the world of coasters before trying something a bit more intense. The ride is great fun for the little ones or just for those not wanting to jump on the likes of *The Hulk* just yet.

Fievel's Playland

A play area for the little ones to let off some steam. There is quite a lot of water here so be sure to bring a change of clothes. There is even a small water slide in this area with dinghies.

E.T. Adventure

Height Restriction: 34 inches (0.87m)
Attraction length: 4 minutes 30 seconds
Express Pass Available: Yes
Average Wait: 20 minutes or less
Lockers required: No

A cute, if ageing, ride where you sit on bicycles like in the E.T. movie and soar through the sky whilst trying to keep E.T. safe. It is a fun little ride with a fairly high capacity and one of the few Universal Studios Florida classics. The ride system is very similar to *Peter Pan's Flight* in Disney's Magic Kingdom Park and it makes for a truly immersive experience. If you do not like heights, avoid this.

Restaurants:

There are no dining locations in this area of the park.

The Wizarding World of Harry Potter – Diagon Alley

This expansion of the Wizarding World of Harry Potter opened in July 2014. It is a great addition to the original Hogsmeade area which already existed in Islands of Adventure.

Diagon Alley is not seen by Muggles (non-Wizards), so the whole of this area of the park is hidden behind a recreation of London's Waterfront. On the waterfront you will find facades of several famous London landmarks.

Here is a glimpse of what this waterfront embankment area looks like:

You will find facades here of: King's Cross Station, Foyles bookstore on Charing Cross Road, Leicester Square tube station, Wyndham's Theatre and houses on Grimmauld Place – number 12 is the home of the Black family in the books and films.

Hidden secret: One cool feature of the waterfront is on the 12 Grimmauld Place building. If you look carefully at the windows above the door, every once in a while the curtain of one of them will open and Kreature, the house elf from the Harry Potter series, will peer outside at the muggles.

As well as the detailed facades, in front of Wyndham's Theatre visitors see the Statue of Eros, and the Purple Knight Bus. This Knight Bus features an interactive shrunken head experience as seen in the Prisoner of Azkaban film – more on this later in this section.

Visitors enter Diagon Alley through the façade of Leicester Square tube station and transition into the Wizarding World by a series of walls with strange brick shapes and sound effects.

Once inside, Diagon Alley is laid out before you with shops on both sides, and the iconic Gringotts Bank at the end. Gringotts Bank houses the premiere attraction of Diagon Alley, which we will come to later in the guide. It even features a fire-breathing dragon on the roof.

Shops:

There is an incredible variety of shops in the main stretch of Diagon Alley.

- **Quality Quidditch Supplies** – This shop carries Quidditch themed merchandise, including apparel, hats and pendants, as well as brooms, Golden Snitches, Bludgers and bats and Quaffles.
- **Weasleys' Wizard Weezes** – This three-story shop features all kinds of prank-filled items and toys, as well as novelty items and magic tricks, including Extendable Ears, Decoy Detonators and Fangled Flyers.
- **Madam Malkin's** – Find all variety of wizard themed clothing here including complete Hogwarts school uniforms, with ties, robes, scarves, and more on offer. Other apparel and jewelry themed to the four school houses is also offered.
- **Ollivander's (show experience and shop)** – This experience is very similar to Ollivander's in Hogsmeade. The difference is that here there are several rooms performing shows simultaneously and therefore waits are almost always very short. Guests can purchase a unique Ollivander's wand, or choose from character replica wands.
- **Wiseacre's Wizarding Equipment** – Find all kinds of wizardry essentials here. From hourglasses to compasses, and telescopes to binoculars. Plus themed apparel.
- **Wands by Gregorovitch** – Purchase your wands from this legendary wandmaker's shop.
- **Shutterbuttons** – Get a personalized video of you in the Wizarding World. Stand in front of a green screen and perform various actions and get a "moving picture" made just like the newspapers in Harry Potter. Pricing is $49.95. Up to 4 people can partake in the experience together. You will be supplied with Potter robes, but you must bring your own wand if you want one in the video.

Restaurants:

Fans of the young boy wizard will definitely not go hungry in Diagon Alley due to the wealth of dining options available:

- **Leaky Cauldron** – Quick service location. Accepts Universal Dining Plan. This location serves tradition English fare such as Banger's and Mash, cottage Pie, Toad in the Hole, Fish and Chips and much more. Entrees are priced at $9 to $20.

- **Florean Fortescue's Ice Cream** – Quick service location. Serves themed ice cream and other cold treats. Does not accept the Universal Dining Plan. Ice cream flavors include: Granny Smith, Earl Grey and Lavender, Clotted Cream, Orange Marmalade, and Butterbeer flavor just to name a few. This location also serves breakfast items and pastries in the morning. Ice creams priced at $5 to $13. (We highly recommend the Butterbeer ice cream – its delicious, but toppings are not allowed)

Guests can explore all these locations, but Diagon Alley also includes a number of shop fronts that guests cannot step inside of. These still make for fantastic photo opportunities. Get snaps with the offices of the Daily Prophet, Broomstix, Flourish and Blotts and many others.

Knockturn Alley:

Running alongside Diagon Alley, is the darker "Knockturn Alley", described as a "gloomy back street" by Universal. The shops and storefronts here are filled with items related to Dark Magic. The flagship store in this area is **Borgin and Burkes**, which sells dark items such as Death Eater masks, skulls and other sinister objects – plus make sure to check out the vanishing cabinet.

This area is covered so as to look continually dark and give a nighttime atmosphere, so expect it to be popular when one of Orlando's frequent rain showers makes its appearance.

Be sure to look out for the animated "Wanted" posters of the Death Eaters, and the window with the tarantulas on it might give you a bit more than you bargained for if you get too close.

There are also many interactive wand experiences available in this area of the land (more on these later). Two other streets in Diagon Alley have themed shop fronts and interactive wand touches – Horizont Alley and Carkitt Market.

Attractions:
Harry Potter and the Escape from Gringotts

Height Restriction: 42 inches (1.07m)
Attraction length: 5 minutes
Express Pass Available: No
Lockers required: Yes
Average Waits: 30 to 60 minutes

Outside the bank, marvel at the fire-breathing dragon on the roof. Then, once inside the bank, you prepare for the experience of a lifetime. The queue line begins by going past several iconic locations: you will see the animatronic Goblins hard at work in the grand marble lobby, as well as wizard vaults and go through a security area (where you have your photo taken), and even get to board a huge elevator. Just like the 'Harry Potter and the Forbidden Journey' ride in Islands of Adventure, this attraction's queue line is as much of an experience as the ride itself. The storyline begins to unfold as you see signs of Harry, Ron and Hermione discussing their plans.

The ride itself is a rollercoaster-type attraction which is described as "multidimensional" by Universal and mixes a variety of real world elements with footage on huge screens, much like 'Forbidden Journey'. Although there are drops and turns (but no loops or inversions) in the layout, think of this more as a 3D-experience ride than a rollercoaster – it is more *Transformers* than *The Incredible Hulk*, but at the same time completely unlike both of these. The ride features 4K-high definition technology as well as 3D screens, with glasses being worn by riders.

Storyline – spoiler alert: The ride is inspired by the final film "Harry Potter and the Deathly Hallows – Part 2," and a pivotal scene where Harry, Ron and Hermione break into Gringotts bank to steal a powerful Horcrux that will help them defeat Lord Voldemort. On Harry Potter and the Escape from Gringotts, you will encounter the trio during this quest – but expect to meet some dangerous creatures and malicious villains as well! During the ride you will come face to face with Bellatrix Lestrange, security trolls, fire breathing dragons and even Voldemort himself.

A single rider line is available, but it skips all indoor scenes and leads directly to the loading area. Remember that the queue line scenes are a significant part of the experience here but if all you want is the ride itself, the single rider line can save you a significant amount of time.

Ollivanders:

Height Restriction: None
Attraction length: 3 to 4 minutes
Express Pass Available: No
Average Wait: Under 10 minutes

Technically this is a pre-show to a shop. Get in line and you will go into Ollivanders in small groups of about 25 people. One person in the group will be chosen by the wandmaster to find the right wand for them. Eventually the right one is found and they are given the opportunity to buy it when the group is moved to the shop area next door. This is a fantastic experience that we highly recommend you visit. It is suitable for people of all ages. The queue lines at this Ollivanders move much more quickly than the one in Islands of Adventure, as there are three show rooms here instead of one in the other land.

Interactive Wand Experiences:

An interactive wand experience is available at the Wizarding World, both at Diagon Alley and Hogsmeade – this additional experience launched with the opening of Diagon Alley. In order to participate, guests must purchase an interactive wand from the Wizarding World's shops. These are priced at $48, around $8 more than the non-interactive wands.

Once you have purchased a wand, look for the bronze medallions embedded in the streets that mark the various locations where you can cast spells. A map of the locations is included with each wand.

Once you are standing on one of the medallions, just perform the correct spell. Simply draw the shape of the spell in the air with your wand and saying the name of the spell – all this is shown on the medallions on the floor – and there are usually Universal's Wizards there to help. Then, watch the magic come to life.

This is a really fun bit of extra entertainment, especially as the wands can be reused again and again during future visits.

Kings Cross Station and the Hogwarts Express:

Height Restriction: None
Attraction length: About 5 minutes in each direction.
Express Pass Available: No
Lockers required: No
Average Waits: 15 to 60 minutes (A park-to-park ticket is required)

The final area and attraction to explore in the Diagon Alley expansion is Kings Cross Station. Guests can enter Kings Cross Station and admire it in all its beauty – faithfully recreated – and then break through the platform's wall and This on platform 9 ¾ where you will be able to catch the Hogwarts Express. which will transport you through the countryside to Hogsmeade Station (located at Universal's Islands of Adventure). The journey lasts several minutes and as you look out of the windows of the train you will see stories unfold – all on a real full-sized train, with compartments to sit in just like Harry and his friends did in the films.

During the journey you can gaze out of the windows and see Hagrid on his motorcycle, the English countryside, Buckbeak the Hippogriff, the purple Knightbus, the Weasley twins on brooms, and even Dementors. There are many more surprises in store, of course. Each of the Hogwarts Express trains seats 200 passengers, with trips in each direction being unique.

Once you hop off the train at Hogsmeade you will be able to explore the area and the Harry Potter themed attractions, including the incredible 'Harry Potter and the Forbidden Journey' ride. This train is the first ever inter-park ride!

Important: In order to experience the Hogwarts Express, attraction visitors must have a park-to-park ticket. A single park ticket will not allow visitors to experience this ride – guests with this ticket can, of course, experience each of the theme parks' Wizarding Worlds on separate days but they cannot use the Hogwarts Express to travel between them.

Diagon Alley Live Entertainment:

Diagon Alley features several pieces of live entertainment in the same way that Hogsmeade does in Islands of Adventure. Inside the Carkitt Market area, two shows are performed daily:

The first show brings to life two fables from **The Tales of Beedle the Bard** – "The Fountain of Fair Fortune" and "The Tale of the Three Brothers" (which was featured in the seventh film). Performed by a troupe of four from the Wizarding Academy of Dramatic Arts, this trunk show uses scenic pieces, props and puppetry fabricated by Emmy-award-winning designer Michael Curry.

The second show features a musical performance by **The Singing Sorceress: Celestina Warbeck and the Banshees**. With a whole lot of soul, this swinging show features never-before heard songs including "A Cauldron Full Of Hot, Strong Love," "You Stole My Cauldron But You Can't Have My Heart" and "You Charmed The Heart Right Out Of Me" – all titles created by J.K. Rowling. The lyrics also contain never-before-revealed information about Celestina's wand – written by J.K. Rowling for Pottermore.

As well as the live stage shows, the area features a host of other interactive experiences. Just outside Diagon Alley itself, by the London waterfront, you will find the **Knight Bus** and its two permanent occupants: a shrunken head and the Knight Bus Conductor, who will be more than happy to chat, joke around and take photos with you.

If you fancy owning some Wizarding currency then be sure to stop by **Gringotts Money Exchange** where you are able to exchange your Muggle currency for Wizarding Bank Notes, which can be used within both Diagon Alley and Hogsmeade (as well as the rest of the two theme parks) to purchase snacks and items from the shops. The shops accept regular US dollars too but these Wizarding bank notes can make for a cool and cheap souvenir.

Character Meets and Drinks:

To maintain the integrity of the Harry Potter areas, J.K. Rowling specified that no branded drinks be sold in both Wizarding Worlds – so you will find no Coca Cola products here. You will only find Harry Potter branded drinks such as Butterbeer, water and some fruit squashes. You are, of course, free to buy any drink elsewhere in the park and bring it into the Wizarding World.

J.K. Rowling also required that there be no characters to meet here – so you will not be able to meet Harry, Hermione, Hagrid, Draco, Ron or any other characters from the films in the Wizarding World. An exception to this is the Knight Bus driver outside Diagon Alley.

Crowd Control Measures and The Return Ticket system:

J. K. Rowling, the author of the Harry Potter books, specifically requested that the buildings in the Wizarding World be made the scale. As such, both Diagon Alley and Hogsmeade are relatively small and can only accommodate a certain number of people – Hogsmeade, much more so than Diagon Alley.

During periods of peak attendance at the park, Universal Orlando may implement crowd control measures. There are two main measures that may be used: a stand-by line to enter the Wizarding Worlds, and a return ticket system. It is not possible to know in advance if either of these systems will be used – if you are visiting around a major holiday, though, there is a high chance.

With the stand-by line you simply wait in a queue line to get into either Diagon Alley or Hogsmeade. Once you reach the end of the line you enter the land.

With the return ticket system, you go to a kiosk, select a return time and get a ticket to come back and enter the Wizarding World immediately. This works similarly to FastPass+ at Walt Disney World. Only one person needs to go to the kiosks and

Return tickets kiosks are located at Jurassic Park at Islands of Adventure, and next to Fear Factor Live at Universal Studios Florida. Team Members will be available to direct you.

If on the day you are visiting both systems are in use, we recommend getting a return ticket as you can then use the time to ride attractions elsewhere in the park, and then return for immediate entry. If you have an Express Pass, this is useless here, you must still either wait in line or get a return ticket.

On days when crowd control measures are in place, expect very high wait times for all attractions within the land – this means 90 to 120 minutes for the headline attractions, and 60 minutes for everything else. These crowd control measures are merely a way of limiting the number of people in the land.

The system will only be in operation when the lands have reached full capacity. So, you may find that during certain hours you need a return ticket to get in, but not during others. The crowd control measures are also independent between the two parks, so they may in operation at one Wizarding World area but not the other.

Once you are inside one of the Wizarding Worlds, taking the Hogwarts Express to the other does not allow you to bypass this system. This is because both train stations are located outside of the areas subject to crowd controls. For example, you may be in Hogsmeade where there are no crowd control measures in place and get the train to Diagon Alley and Kings Cross. Upon arrival at Kings Cross if the crowd control system is in use you will need to either use the stand-by line or the return ticket system to gain access to the land. This works the other way round too, from Diagon Alley to Hogsmeade.

Since the opening of Diagon Alley in Universal Studios Florida in Summer 2014, crowds are larger there than at Hogsmeade – as such we do not expect this return ticket system to be used in Hogsmeade except in the rarest of occasions. There is, however, a chance that this system may be **used for** Diagon Alley during your visit.

Early Entry:

Staying on site at a Universal resort hotel has numerous benefits – including, notably, early admission into the *WWOHP* one hour before the general public. This also applies to off-site hotels booked as part of a Universal vacation package, which includes park tickets and accommodation together at **www.universalorlandovacations.com** or through an authorized reseller – check to make sure this benefit is included in your package.

The side of the *WWOHP* that is open for early entry changes regularly, check the Universal website to find out if it will be Diagon Alley or Hogsmeade which will be open.

If you do not have Early Park Admission, be at the park turnstiles well before opening as Universal frequently lets guests in up to 30 minutes earlier than the advertised opening time.

Universal Studios Florida Park Entertainment:

Universal Studios Florida is also home to much more live entertainment throughout the day outside Diagon Alley. Character meet and greets can be found throughout the park, there is a daily parade and a nighttime spectacular rounds out the fun.

Universal's Superstar Parade

Expect to see the characters from Despicable Me - including Gru and the Minions, Sponge Bob Squarepants and Dora the Explorer, among other characters in the daily *Universal Superstar Parade*. This parade is great fun for those who are fans of characters. Both the floats and the characters are great to see as they dance along to music.

The parade route starts by the *Universal's Horror Make Up Show* attraction and moves towards the lagoon, past *TRANSFORMERS*, round the front *of Revenge of the Mummy*, down past the Universal Stage and *Despicable Me* and back along Hollywood Boulevard ending next to *Universal's Horror Make Up Show*.

One of the best things about *Universal's Superstar Parade* is that it is nowhere near as crowded as the parades at Disney's theme park - many people simply do not know it exists; many others just go to Universal for the thrills. Having said this, although the parade is enjoyable it is nowhere near the standards of a Disney parade. The parade is performed once each day - the time will be printed on your park map.

Top Tip: Twice per day, before the parade starts there are dance parties hosted by Mel's Drive-In twice. During the dance parties floats and characters from the parade will come out to meet and greet, dance and sign autographs.

Universal's Cinematic Spectacular: 100 Years of Movie Memories

Universal Orlando's way to bid you goodnight is with its "Cinematic Spectacular", a nostalgic viewing of highlights from Universal movies of the last 100 years. The show takes place every evening on the lagoon in the middle of the park and features water screens, a great soundtrack, fountains and fireworks. The show is thematically split up into categories such as comedy and horror, with clips from famous films shown on water curtains.

The 18-minute nighttime show is perhaps more pertinent to adults than children due to the age of some clips. This is also more of a projection show than a fireworks show, with fireworks being few and far between.

If you do want a front row view, then usually turning up 30 minutes before the show's scheduled start time will easily guarantee you a good spot. If you do not fancy waiting that long, then simply turn up a few minutes before show time. There should not be too many people in front of you as there is such a large viewing area.

This is not a Disney or even SeaWorld-quality show in our opinion, and if you have high expectations you will be disappointed. Nevertheless, it is worth a viewing but once you have watched it once, we doubt stick around for it on other days.

There is a dining experience option at Lombard's Seafood Grille which gives you reserved seating for the show but even on peak summer days we never found the area around the lagoon to be crowded to the point where we would consider this necessary. Reservations are required 24 hours in advance. Prices are $44.99 for adults and $12.99 for children and include an appetizer, entrée, dessert and one non-alcoholic beverage, as well as VIP viewing of the nighttime spectacular.

There is an area in the Simpsons Fast Food Boulevard zone that is reserved for VIP viewing of the cinematic spectacular in the evenings. Seating here is priced at $15 and is on offer 45 minutes before the show begins. The price of the VIP area includes gratuity, one cupcake and one non-alcoholic beverages (excluding Flaming Moes), meaning that the effective cost of the seating is about $8. If it is busy and you fancy a dessert this could be a good option for you.

Our favourite view is from the area outside TRANSFORMERS, in our opinion this gives you the best overall view of the show with the screens facing you and the fireworks launched in your line of sight.

Chapter 6

Universal's Islands of Adventure - Park Guide:

Universal's Islands of Adventure opened in 1999 with many famed attractions, instantly putting it on the world theme park map. The true revolution for the park, however, came with the opening of *The Wizarding World of Harry Potter: Hogsmeade* in 2010, and expansion and innovation in the park have not stopped since. In this theme park you will not find 'lands' but 'islands'. Together these islands make up Universal's Islands of Adventure. The park hosted 8.1 million guests in 2014.

Port of Entry

Perhaps the most beautiful entrance to a theme park in America, *Port of Entry* transports you to a different time and place and shows that Universal really *does* think about its theming, despite what some may say. There are no attractions in this area of the park but rather it acts as an entranceway to the Islands of Adventure themselves. You will find many shops and a few places to eat in this area.

To the right of the welcome arch at *Port of Entry* you will find **Guest Services** where you can get help with disability assistance, dining reservations, questions, compliments and complaints. **Lost and Found** is also located here.

Lockers, a **phone card vending machine** and a **payphone** are all located to the left of the archway. **Strollers** and **wheelchair rentals** can also be found here. **First Aid** is located inside the Open Arms Hotel building to the right of the entrance archway. There is another first aid station in The Lost Continent area by the bazaar.

Fun fact: At the wheelchair and stroller rental location look out for a sign which lists the pricing of rentals along with several gag items which have already been "rented out" including a gondola, an aero boat and a rocket car.

Restaurants:

Confisco Grill and Backwater Bar – Table service location. Accepts Universal Dining Plan. Serves wood-oven pizzas, sandwiches, pasta and fajitas. Entrees priced at $9 to $18. The Backwater Bar has a happy hour that runs daily from 4:00pm to 7:00pm (subject to change).

Croissant Moon Bakery – Quick service location. Accepts Universal Dining Plan. Serves continental breakfasts, sandwiches, paninis, cakes and branded coffee. Entrees are priced between $2.50 and $10. Note: This location is not listed on the map – it is on the right hand side of Port of Entry.

Starbucks – Quick service location. Does not accept the Universal Dining Plan. Located right next to Cinnabon.

Seuss Landing

This area is completely themed around the Dr. Seuss books. To add to the look of the area, the theme park designers made sure there were no straight lines anywhere in this land.

Caro-Seuss-el

Height Restriction: None
Capacity: Approximately 1000 guests per hour
Attraction length: 2 minutes
Express Pass Available: Yes
Average Wait: Less than 15 minutes
A classic carrousel type ride themed to the Seuss series of books.

The Cat in the Hat

Height Restriction: 36 inches (0.92m) minimum to ride with an adult, or 48 inches (1.22m) to ride alone
Capacity: 1800 people per hour
Attraction length: 4 minutes
Express Pass Available: Yes
Average Wait: 15 to 45 minutes

A dark ride where you travel through the story of *The Cat in the Hat* with favorite characters, and spin along the way. Admittedly, the ride makes much more sense if you have read the books or seen the films but anyone can appreciate this adventure.

Note: Guests under 36" may not ride. Guests 36" to 48" must ride with a supervising companion. Hand-held infants are not allowed.

One Fish, Two Fish, Red Fish, Blue Fish

Height Restriction: Children under 48 inches (1.22m) must ride with an adult
Capacity: 350 people per hour

Attraction length: 1 minute 30 seconds
Express Pass Available: Yes
Average Wait: 15 to 45 minutes
You have surely seen the classic spinning type rides before, like Dumbo in the Disney parks. This one is similar, yet, it packs a bit of a twist. On this ride, you will want to follow along with what the famous Dr. Seuss song says in order to stay dry. So when you hear "up, up, up" you will want to steer yourself upwards and be as high as you can be to avoid getting soaked. This is a fun twist on what usually can be a bit of a repetitive, unimaginative ride. During colder times the water is turned off.

The High in the Sky Seuss Trolley Train Ride

Height Restriction: 40 inches (1.02m) minimum to ride (must be accompanied) or 48 inches (1.22m) to ride alone
Attraction length: 5 minutes
Express Pass Available: Yes
Average Wait: 15 to 45 minutes
A cute, slow journey across the rooftops in Seuss Landing. Note how there are no straight lines in this area as you go around the crazy land of Dr. Seuss.

If I Ran the Zoo
A play area for kids to run around, designed in a maze-like format. Good for big Dr. Seuss fans with some in-jokes along the way. There is a water area here too to cool down on the classic hot Floridian days.

Restaurants:
Circus McGurks Cafe Stoo-pendous – Quick Service location. Accepts Universal Dining Plan. Serves pizza, pasta, salads, cheeseburgers and chicken. Entrees are priced at $7 to $9.

The Lost Continent

Themed to mythological creatures and legends, this area of the park is home to two big show experiences, **Poseidon's Fury** and **The Eighth Voyage of Sindbad Stunt Show**, as well as the park's acclaimed restaurant **Mythos**.

The Mystic Fountain

This is listed as an attraction on the map, but we would hesitate to really call it one. Essentially, it is a talking, interactive fountain. It is usually very witty and it can be a good source of laughs. Beware, though, the fountain loves to get people wet!

Poseidon's Fury

Height Restriction: None
Attraction length: 15 minutes
Express Pass Available: Yes
Average Wait: 15 to 45 minutes

This attraction is an interesting concept – it is a walk-through live show where your guide takes you deeper and deeper into the Temple of Poseidon. Some cool fire and water effects are used throughout the show but be prepared to stand for an extended period of time as you move from room to room throughout the show. The attraction does look much grander from the outside than it is on the inside. In our opinion it is not worth more than a 30-minute wait. It is a good attraction but if the queues are long come back later in the day.

The Eighth Voyage of Sindbad Stunt Show

Show length: 22 minutes
Express Pass Available: Yes
Average Wait: None. Presented at scheduled times only.

This is an action-packed show with special effects at every opportunity. It is these effects, ironically, that are the main problem with the show for us: the show is just a montage of effects without a decent storyline. If it is raining, this show is a good bit of shelter but otherwise we would recommend giving it a miss. In our opinion, this is the worst attraction in both parks. Note: To those who do not like loud bangs, avoid this show!

Restaurants:

Mythos Restaurant – Table Service location. Accepts Universal Dining Plan. Serves sandwiches, Shortribs, Asian Salmon and Mahi Mahi. Entrees are priced at $13 to $20. This is our favorite restaurant in the park. Note: Mythos is only open for lunch.

Fire Eater's Grill – Quick Service location. Accepts Universal Dining Plan. Serves hot dogs, chicken fingers, grilled gyro and salads. Entrees are priced at $8 to $9. Surprisingly large portions.

Fun fact: Behind Mythos Restaurant there is a bridge. Stand under it and you might just hear a troll!

The Wizarding World of Harry Potter - Hogsmeade

Step into the world of Harry Potter and experience what it is like to visit Hogsmeade - dine there, visit the shops and experience some wild rides. The area is incredibly well themed and Potter fans will be see authenticity unlike anywhere else. Throughout this section you may see The Wizarding World of Harry Potter abbreviated to WWOHP.

To avoid any misconception, we would like to clarify that this is just an island of the park, albeit a very well themed one, and NOT an entire theme park as some of the press have reported in the past. It also existed several years before the Diagon Alley area opened over in Universal Studios Florida. Both the Wizarding World areas are connected by the Hogwarts Express – a real train connecting both theme parks.

Fun fact: The attention to detail in this land is stunning. In the restrooms at the Wizarding World, you can hear Moaning Myrtle, and in the rafters of Three Broomsticks you can see shadows of owls flying about.

Dragon Challenge

Height Restriction: 54 inches (1.37m)
Capacity: 3500 people per hour
Attraction length: 2 minutes 25 seconds
Express Pass Available: Yes
Average Wait: 60 to 90 minutes
Re-themed from *Dueling Dragons* to its current incarnation, the ride layout has remained the same. You will see Ron Weasley's car in the queue, enter Hogwarts and then fly on an incredible inverted coaster. There are actually two coasters here: the Hungarian Horntail and the Chinese Fireball. These is one queue line for both coasters and then at the end it splits: here you choose which you want to ride.

The queue line is immense and going on for what feels like miles but it does move fairly quickly. If you are claustrophobic you should avoid this ride as the queue goes through some very small and tight caves at one point.

Top Tip 1: During the first section of the Dragon Challenge queue when you are outside, there is a viewing area – here you can get some great photos of Hogwarts, perfectly framed. Alternatively, it is a great place to watch the shows performed in this area of the park with no crowds.

Triwizard Spirit Rally

This show is a six-minute dance contest between two competing wizard schools: men versus women. The men's routine involves complex sword-fighting techniques, whilst the ladies dazzle with their ribbons and acrobatics. It is a nice bit of street/stage entertainment and a great photo opportunity.

Frog Choir

A nine-minute series of songs inspired by the the Harry Potter movies performed by Hogwarts students and their frogs - all done acapella with voices and no instruments, there is an almost beat-box flair to this show and it is a great piece of live entertainment.

Flight of the Hippogriff

Height Restriction: 36 inches (0.92m)
Capacity: 650 people per hour
Attraction length: 1 minute 5 seconds
Express Pass Available: Yes
Average Wait: 45 to 60 minutes
A small rollercoaster where you soar on a Hippogriff and go past Hagrid's hut. Good family fun and a good starter coaster before putting your children on the likes of *The Hulk*.

Harry Potter and the Forbidden Journey

Height Restriction: 48 inches (1.22m)
Capacity: 2800 people per hour
Attraction length: 5 minutes
Express Pass Available: No
Average Wait: 30 to 60 minutes

A truly groundbreaking ride featuring projection screens, hugely flexible ride vehicles and an incredibly detailed queue. The opening of this attraction was a turning point in Universal Orlando's history, cementing its spot as one of the world's best theme park resorts. The ride vehicles move effortlessly from scene to scene, with incredible technology and an interesting storyline. The moment your enchanted bench first takes off is breathtaking. The queue line is almost an attraction in itself.

If you do not wish to experience the ride, you can still explore the inside of Hogwarts castle, simply ask one of the team members for the Tour Only entrance – this allows you to skip the locker line and bring cameras to take photos of the incredibly well-themed interior.

There is a single rider line available too. This can cut down wait times significantly; expected single rider waits are usually about 50-75% shorter than the standard wait time in our experience, though mileage may vary.

Warning: We have found that this ride creates an incredible amount of mental strain on your mind due to the simulated sensations you feel and the realism of the screens in front of you. This means that if you ride it more than once in a row you are likely to feel unwell. Almost everyone we have spoken to says the same thing, even if they can deal with riding rollercoasters back to back, this ride is a whole different beast.

Hidden Secret: When you are in Dumbledore's office hearing his speech, take a look at the books on the wall to the right of him. Once in a while, one of the books may just do something very magical.

Hidden Secret 2: Look at the moving portraits of the four founders of Hogwarts; each of them is holding a Horcrux used to defeat Voldemort in the films and books.

Hogsmeade Station and the Hogwarts Express:

Height Restriction: None
Attraction length: About 5 minutes in each direction.
Express Pass Available: No
Lockers required: No
Average Waits: 15 to 60 minutes (A park-to-park ticket is required)
The final area and attraction to explore in this area is Hogsmeade's station giving access to the Hogwarts Express. Guests can enter Hogsmeade Station and admire it in all its beauty and catch the Hogwarts Express, which will transport you through the countryside to Kings Cross Station (located at Universal Studios Florida park). The journey lasts several minutes and as you look out of the windows of the train you will see stories unfold – all on a real full-sized train, with compartments to sit in just like Harry and his friends did in the films.

Once you hop off the train at King's Cross you will be in London. From there you can enter Diagon Alley and explore the Harry Potter themed attractions there, including the innovative 'Harry Potter and the Escape from Gringotts' attraction!

Important: Guests must have a park-to-park ticket to experience the Hogwarts Express attraction. A single park ticket will not allow visitors to experience the ride.

Ollivanders

Height Restriction: None
Capacity: 250 people per hour
Attraction length: 3 to 4 minutes
Express Pass Available: No
Average Wait: 15 to 45 minutes

This is very similar to the Ollivanders attraction at Diagon Alley. This version was around first, though. Here there is only a single show room meaning that wait times can get unnecessarily long. The same experience is available at Diagon Alley but with much shorter waits.

Note: This is not listed as an attraction on the park map. There is no wait time sign at the front of the queue line either and the entrance is not very clear. The entrance is the railings to the left-hand side of door to Ollivander's. It is easy to estimate how long the queue is: do a quick headcount of the people in line in front of you - the wait is about 6 minutes for every 25 people ahead of you in the line.

Restaurants:

The restaurants in Hogsmeade are incredibly well-themed. We highly recommend you take a look inside the Hog's Head and Three Broomsticks, even if you do not plan to eat there. Three Broomsticks in particular is an absolute masterpiece that should not be missed. Look upstairs in the rafters to see some cool details.

- **Hog's Head** – Quick Service location. Does not accept the Universal Dining Plan. This pub is located in the same building as the Three Broomsticks. Serves alcoholic beer, a selection of spirits, non-alcoholic Butterbeer and juices. Drinks are priced at $2.50 to $7.

- **Three Broomsticks** - Quick Service location. Accepts Universal Dining Plan. Serves breakfast meals inspired from around the world. At lunch and dinner you will find Cornish pasties, fish & chips, Shepard's pie, smoked turkey legs, rotisserie smoked chicken and spareribs. Entrees are priced at $8 to $15.

Shops:

The shops and merchandise in the Wizarding World are just as much of an experience as some of the rides. Be sure to step inside to admire the detail, and maybe even purchase a souvenir or two. Shops in the area include:

- **Filch's Emporium of Confiscated Goods** – This is the exit gift shop to the Harry Potter and the Forbidden Journey attraction. Inside you will find everything from themed t-shirts to hats and scarves, mugs, photo frames and trinkets. It has almost everything a Harry Potter fan could ever want. The shop also contains a few items themed to dark magic.

- **Honeydukes** – For those who have a sweet tooth, make sure to visit Honeydukes. You will find everything from love potion sweets to chocolate frogs (with collectable trading cards), and tons of other candy.
- **The Owlery and Dervish & Banges** – This is the place to come for your Harry Potter wands. There are also Horcrux replicas and even a scaled down model of the Hogwarts Express. Clothing is also sold here, as well as stationary and Quidditch items – you can even bag yourself a golden snitch!
- **The Owl Post** – A real post office where your letters or postcards can be sent to friends and family – these will get a Hogsmeade postmark and a Harry Potter stamp. You will also find stationary on sale here, as well as owl toys.

Note: Official Harry Potter branded wands are expensive – expect to pay $40 a piece for regular wands and $48 for interactive ones.

Jurassic Park:

Since the first film became a classic in 1993, children and adults alike have dreamed of visiting this magical world of dinosaurs. Universal's Islands of Adventure allows you do just that at Jurassic Park.

There are several photo opportunities located throughout the land including jeeps with dinosaurs next to them. These jeeps are the actual ones which were used in the first movie!

Camp Jurassic

A play area themed around the Jurassic Park films. We definitely recommend exploring the area as the detail is just incredible – what's more, this isn't one of those playground areas only reserved to children, here anyone or any age can explore the area and all it has to offer, from the caves to the water jets and the treetop platforms to the slides.

Fun fact: Stepping on some of the dinosaur footprints on the ground in this area, will emit a roaring dinosaur sound.

Pteranodon Flyers

Height Restriction: The minimum height is 36 inches (0.92m). Guests over 56 inches (1.43m) must be accompanied by someone under 36 inches (0.92m) to ride.

Attraction length: 1 minute

Express Pass Available: Yes

Average Wait: 45 to 75 minutes

Soar above Jurassic Park on a winged dinosaur. This is the only attraction in the park to have such a restrictive set of requirements. In order for an adult (or anyone over 56 inches) to ride they must be accompanied by someone under 36 inches tall. This really limits the number of guests who can experience this attraction. Queues are very slow moving so if you will be riding this, come first or last in the day.

Raptor Encounter

This is an opportunity to meet and take photos with a real life raptor. Be careful they are unpredictable and loud but there are always Universal Team Members on hand should anything get out of hand. Being dangerous, the raptors aren't walking around the land but instead you'll find them in a fixed position and they'll stick their heads out through a gap in the fence so you can get some great photos.

You can take photos yourself or there are also Photo Connect photographers present. At the time of writing, appearance times are not posted on the park map but the raptors are usually available to meet between 11:00am and 4:30pm.

Jurassic Park River Adventure

Height Restriction: 42 inches (1.07m)
Capacity: 3000 people per hour.
Attraction length: 5 minutes 30 seconds
Express Pass Available: Yes
Average Wait: 45 to 90 minutes

Step into the world of Jurassic Park on a river boat, glide past huge dinosaurs, and enter through enormous doors just like in the movies. However, this calm river adventure will soon change course. Watch out for the T-Rex before you come splashing down an 85-foot drop! A single rider line is available at this attraction.

Top Tip: You won't stay dry wherever you sit on this ride, but the driest seats are on the back row.

Note: Lockers are not compulsory for this ride, so be prepared to pay $4 for 90 minutes of locker time. There are also giant human-sized dryers priced at around $5 but we find these to be ineffective and a waste of money.

Jurassic Park Discovery Center

An exploration area where you can see models dinosaurs, play dinosaur-themed carnival-style games, learn about DNA sequencing, and witness a dinosaur birth. The main part of the Discovery Center is downstairs in the building.

Top Tip: Exit out the back doors and you will find an outdoor patio area which is a great place to take long-shot photos of *Islands of Adventure* – you will get great views of *Seuss Landing* and *Marvel Super Hero Island* in particular.

Restaurants:

The Burger Digs – Quick Service location. Accepts Universal Dining Plan. Serves burgers, chicken tenders and chicken sandwiches. Entrees are priced at $8 to $10.

Thunder Falls Terrace – Quick Service location. Accepts Universal Dining Plan. Serves cheeseburgers, ribs, smoked turkey legs, wraps, and rotisserie chicken. Entrees are priced at $9 to $16. The portion sizes are large at this restaurant.

Skull Island – Reign of Kong (Opens Summer 2016):

A King Kong attraction has long been rumored for *Islands of Adventure* but now its really happening – and it is opening this summer at Islands of Adventure. Skull Island: Reign of Kong will be a multi-sensory, multi-dimensional new ride where passengers will board 4x4 vehicles. The ride will turn into a "fight for survival as you encounter creatures of unknown origin and even the great Kong himself".

The façade of the ride building is immense and we are very excited for this new addition to *Islands of Adventure*.

Unfortunately, Universal Orlando has not released any more details about the attraction at this time. We also do not know whether this will be classified as an entire new land or just the addition of an attraction to the Jurassic Park section of the park. We also do not know if this attraction will be getting Express Pass access.

Toon Lagoon:

Toon Lagoon is an entire land dedicated to water – with the park's two wettest water attractions being located here, as well as water elements everywhere throughout the area. The characters in the land are based on those created by Jay Ward and the King Features Syndicate.

Dudley Do-Right's Ripsaw Falls

Height Restriction: 44 inches (1.12m)
Attraction length: 7 minutes
Express Pass Available: Yes
Average Wait: 45 to 75 minutes

Want a water ride that gets you absolutely soaked? You should give this one a try. The ride contains a well-themed interior and culminates in several drops with a final rollercoaster-like splashdown making sure you leave thoroughly drenched. The ride reaches a top speed of 45mph (over 70 km/h), so you get a great thrill too! A single rider line is available at this attraction.

Me Ship, The Olive

A play area for the kids to run around in. This is usually a very quiet area of the park and a great place to have a break from the crowds. For those who like causing chaos, there are free water cannons on the top level of the ship to spray guests on the Popeye water ride below.

Top Tip: The top level of this attraction gives you some great views of the park and is a good place to get photos.

Fun fact: On the right hand side of this attraction there is a trail. Follow it for some hilarious gags, such as a "school" of fish.

Popeye & Bluto's Bilge-Rat Barges

Height Restriction: 42 inches (1.07m)
Capacity: 2400 people per hour
Attraction length: 6 minutes
Express Pass Available: Yes
Average Wait: 45 to 90 minutes

If you thought you got wet on Dudley Do-Right's, you surely have not seen this ride yet. Popeye's will make sure you will come out drenched from head to toe. This is by far the wettest water ride in all of Orlando and it is a whole lot of fun along the way – Universal has come up with some pretty creative ways to get you wet.

Restaurants:

Blondie's – Quick Service location. Accepts Universal Dining Plan. Serves sandwiches, made to order subs and hot dogs. Entrees are priced at $9 to $9.50.

Comic Strip Cafe – Quick Service location. Accepts Universal Dining Plan. Serves Chinese beef and broccoli, chilidogs, sandwiches, fish & chips, pizza and spaghetti and meatballs. Entrees are priced at $7.50 to $14.

Marvel Super Hero Island

This island contains two of our favourite attractions in all of Universal Orlando – Spider-Man and The Hulk, as well as great comic book theming, places to eat and shop and other attractions. You will often find Marvel characters meeting and greeting guests in this area of the park.

The Amazing Adventures of Spider-Man

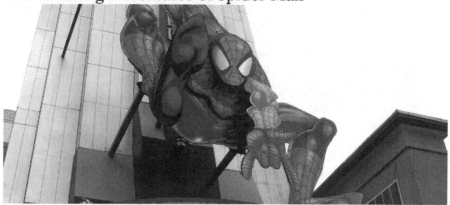

Height Restriction: 40 inches (1.02m)
Attraction length: 5 minutes
Express Pass Available: Yes
Average Wait: 45 to 75 minutes

One of the most groundbreaking rides in the world, *Spider-Man* is a world-class attraction which incorporates projection screens with real world elements like never seen before. More than a decade after its opening, the attraction has not aged a single bit, as it has been updated with 4K and 3D technology creating higher resolution images and the storyline works as well as it ever has.

The ride, which still wins awards every year, is a fun experience swinging around New York City with Spider-Man. This is an absolute must-do at the park.

This ride operates a single rider's line which usually can save you a lot of time.

The Incredible Hulk Coaster (Closed until Summer 2016)

Height Restriction: 54 inches (1.37m)
Capacity: 1920 people per hour
Attraction length: 2 minutes 15 seconds
Express Pass Available: Yes
Average Wait: 30 to 90 minutes

Winner of numerous awards, the Incredible Hulk Coaster is our favorite rollercoaster in all of Orlando. It is a truly outstanding thrill with huge loops, an underground section, and non-stop fun from the moment you are launched out of the tunnel until you are back at the station. There is a hidden single rider line at this attraction, which you should ask the ride attendant at the front to use – the waits are often short as it is not signposted.

Important: This attraction closed in September 2015 and will be closed until Summer 2016 for an extended refurbishment. Universal is rebuilding the entire track, and will be enhancing the storyline and ride vehicles. There is no set reopening date at the time of writing – just Summer 2016.

Doctor Doom's Fearfall

Height Restriction: 52 inches (1.32m)
Capacity: 1600 people per hour
Attraction length: Less than 45 seconds
Express Pass Available: Yes
Average Wait: 45 to 60 minutes

Love drop towers? Then you will adore this ride. Doctor Doom needs your screams for power, so to get them he shoots you up in the air – and he definitely gets more than enough power. This attraction operates a single rider's line – ask for it at the entrance.

Fun fact: Look on the ground outside the attraction for chalk outlines of the Fantastic Four. They, too, went on the ride and came plummeting to the ground, landing where the outlines are. A subtle feature, but really cool.

Storm Force Accelatron

Height Restriction: An adult must accompany those under 48 inches (1.22m)
Attraction length: 2 minutes
Express Pass Available: Yes
Average Wait: Less than 15 minutes
A standard teacup style ride themed to Marvel super hero, Storm.

Restaurants:

Captain America Diner – Quick Service location. Accepts Universal Dining Plan. Serves cheeseburgers, chicken sandwiches, chicken fingers and salads. Entrees priced $8 to $10.50.
Cafe 4 – Quick Service location. Accepts Universal Dining Plan. Serves pizza, pasta, sandwiches and salads. Entrees are priced at $6 to $9.

Universal's Islands of Adventure Live Entertainment:
There are no daily fireworks shows or parades at this park. You will often find characters throughout the various lands, in particular in Seuss Landing and Marvel Superhero Island. There are no Harry Potter characters in Hogsmeade.

Chapter 7

Universal CityWalk:

Universal's CityWalk is located just outside the theme parks, and within walking distance to all the on-site hotels. There are shops, restaurants, bars, cinemas and clubs.

Unlike *Disney Springs*, *CityWalk* has more of an adult feel to it, particularly at nighttime when there is a heavy focus on the club-like atmosphere. It still, however, manages to still keep a fun and friendly atmosphere no matter the time of day. Like *Disney Springs*, there is no admission required to enter *CityWalk* - anyone can explore the area for free. Parking, however, is charged before 6:00pm considering you will park at the main Universal parking garages – there is no other parking.

To get details on restaurant and attraction operating hours, recorded information is available by calling (407) 363-8000.

Guest Services is well signposted and is located next to the **restrooms**. Also located nearby is **First Aid**.

From CityWalk you can catch complimentary boats to Royal Pacific Resort, Portofino Bay Hotel, and Hard Rock Hotel. You can also walk to all the on-site hotels. Room keys are not necessary to board the boat service most of the day but these will be asked for during the late hours.

Dining:

CityWalk is filled with unique dining experiences allowing you to have a taste of Italy, New Orleans, Jamaica and the US all in one place. This section helps you choose where you should eat on your next visit. Note that entree prices quoted in this section are for adult meals; children's meals will often be significantly cheaper.

There are numerous quick service dining options:

Auntie Anne's Pretzel Rolls – Accepts Universal Dining Plan (snacks). Serves soft pretzels. Pretzel and a drink combos are priced at $6 to $8.
Bread Box Handcrafted Sandwiches – Accepts Universal Dining Plan. Serves sandwiches and salads. Entrees priced at $6 to $8.
Burger King 'Whopper Bar' – Does not accept Universal Dining Plan. Serves burgers, wraps and sandwiches.
Cold Stone Creamery – Accepts Universal Dining Plan (snacks). Serves ice cream priced at $4.50 to $7.
Cinnabon – Accepts Universal Dining Plan (snacks and beverages). Serves cinnamon rolls and ice cream. Ice creams are priced at $5 to $9.50.
Fusion Bistro Sushi & Sake Bar – Does not accept Universal Dining Plan. Serves sushi and sake, as well as drinks.
Hot Dog Hall of Fame – Accepts Universal Dining Plan. Serves hot dogs. Entrees are priced at $7 to $13.
Menchie's Frozen Yogurt – Does not accept Universal Dining Plan. Serves frozen yogurt priced at $0.59 per ounce (28g).
Moe's Southwest Grill – Does not accept Universal Dining Plan. Serves burritos, tacos, fajitas and other southwest dishes. Entrees are priced at $4 to $8.50.
Panda Express – Does not accept Universal Dining Plan. Serves Chinese food.
Starbucks Coffee – Accepts Universal Dining Plan for selected snacks and beverages only. Serves coffees, ice-based drinks, sandwiches and pastries.

There are many table service dining options at CityWalk:
Antojitos Authentic Mexican Food – Accepts Universal Dining Plan. Serves Mexican-style food. Entrees are priced at $14 to $29.
Bob Marley – A Tribute to Freedom – Accepts Universal Dining Plan. Serves Jamaican-style dishes. Entrees are priced at $9 to $17.
Bubba Gump Shrimp Co – Does not accept Universal Dining Plan. Serves seafood and other dishes. Entrees are priced at $11 to $27.
The Cowfish Sushi Burger bar – Accepts Universal Dining Plan. Serves burgers and sushi. Entrees are priced at $10 to $27.

Emeril's Restaurant Orlando – Does not accept Universal Dining Plan. Serves Louisiana-style food. Entrees are priced at $11 to $39.

Hard Rock Cafe Orlando – Does not accept Universal Dining Plan. Serves burgers, steaks, ribs and other American-style food. Entrees are priced at $10 to $35.

Jimmy Buffet's Margaritaville – Accepts Universal Dining Plan. Serves Floridian and Caribbean inspired food. Entrees priced at $11 to $39.

NBC Sports Grill & Brew – Does not accept Universal Dining Plan. Sports-bar style setting with 100 TV screens. Serves salads, and American-style food. Entrees are priced at $10 to $45.

Red Oven Pizza Bakery – Accepts Universal Dining Plan. Serves pizza and salads. Whole pies are priced at $12 to $14. Hands down the best pizza at Universal Orlando Resort.

Pat O' Briens – Accepts Universal Dining Plan. A music venue that serves food. Serves New Orleans-style dishes. Entrees are priced at $10 to $15.

Vivo Italian Kitchen – Accepts Universal Dining Plan. Serves Italian food. Entrees are priced at $11 to $33.

Reservations for table service establishments can be made by calling (407) 224-3663 on by visiting opentable.com. Emeril's reservations are made directly by calling (407) 224-2424. Hard Rock Café Orlando priority seating can be requested online.

If you want to combine a meal at select locations with a Party Pass (more information on this later) you can do so for about $21 including tax and gratuity.

A meal plus mini-golf deal is also available for about $4 more, including tax and gratuity, and includes a meal at a select CityWalk location, and 18 holes of mini-golf at the Hollywood Drive-In course.

Top Tip 1: Most establishments have happy hours throughout the day and evening when drinks and snacks can be obtained at significant discounts. These vary from location to location so simply ask the staff for details.

Top Tip 2: Want free CityWalk valet parking? Most restaurants will validate your ticket for a two-hour stay between the hours of 11:00am to 2:00pm Monday to Friday. Emeril's will validate your ticket at any time. Tipping the valets is still customary.

Top Tip 3: Ask for the free VIBE tour of the restaurant and get an insight into the memorabilia and décor of the café, as well as much more. Available daily from 2:00pm to 9:00pm, simply ask inside.

Movie theatre/cinema:

CityWalk features an AMC Universal Cineplex with 20 screens, including one that shows films in IMAX and IMAX 3D.

Tickets prices vary depending on the time of day and several other factors. A general ticket for an adult is priced at $10.00 for shows before 3:55pm and $11.60 from then onwards. Children pay $8.40 all day. "AM" Cinema showings on weekends and holidays before midday are $6.50. Senior tickets for those aged 60 and over are charged at $8.40 to $10.00. Annual pass holders get $3 off two tickets for showings after 4:00pm.

There are upcharges for non-standard tickets. These are: $4 for a 3D movie, $5 for IMAX and $6 for IMAX-3D.

You can save by combining a standard movie ticket and a meal at select CityWalk restaurants. The price is $21.95 including tax and gratuity.

Mini Golf:

"Hollywood Drive-In Golf" is an adventure golf location with two different courses - one themed to sci-fi ("Invaders from Planet Putt"), the other themed to horror movies ("The Haunting of Ghostly Greens"). The sounds, special effects, lighting and theming truly immerse you in the miniature world you are in. The price for one course is $15 per adult and $13 per child. A single course will take between 35 and 45 minutes to complete with each being made up of 18 holes. The entrance is located next to the AMC Cineplex box office. If you play both courses you will receive a T-shirt as a souvenir. Discounts for Florida residents, military, seniors, AAA members and Universal annual pass holders are available.

The mini-golf location is open from 9:00am to 2:00am daily.

Top Tip: Get your mini-golf tickets in advance at http://www.hollywooddriveingolf.com and save up to 13% per ticket— you must book these at least one day in advance.

Nighttime entertainment - Blue Man Group:

The world famous *Blue Man Group* is the staple nighttime show at Universal. The Blue Men create live music with makeshift instruments in a fun and hilarious musical adventure.

The best seats can be had as close to the front as possible and towards the center. The show lasts 1 hour 45 minutes and has no interval. The show schedules change daily with no fixed start times and there are between 1 and 3 shows per day, with shows starting between 3:00pm and 9:00pm.

Ticket prices vary depending on the day of the week. The following prices (tax excluded) are valid from Sunday to Thursday — add $10 per adult and $5 per child for Friday and Saturday shows. Higher prices also apply daily during peak seasons.

	Tier 1	Tier 2	Poncho	Premium
Adult	$70	$85	$95	$105
Child	$30	$37.50	$42.50	$47.50

A VIP experience is available for an additional supplement of $20 per ticket. It includes 2 drinks (alcoholic or non-alcoholic), access to the Bluephoria lounge 45 minutes before and after the show, a meet and greet with a Blue Man and a signed photo.

Tickets can be purchased at the box office or by calling 407-BLUEMAN (407-258-3626) or online at www.blueman.com. Pre-purchasing tickets can save you up to $10 per ticket. An Annual Passholder discount is available with tickets starting at $60 for adults and $30 for children, plus tax.

Money-Saving Tips: Students with a college ID or an ISIC card can get "rush" day-of tickets for $34 – there is a limit of two per ID. AAA members can get a discount by showing their membership card. Military members can also get a discount, visit your local MWR, ITT, and ITR offices for details and to purchase. Buying in advance online will save you up to $10 per ticket.

Shopping:

If you fancy a spot of shopping, there are plenty of places to visit including: Fossil, Fresh Produce, Quiet Flight Surf Shop, Element, The Island Clothing Store, a large Universal Studios Store (where you can get theme park gear without having to enter the theme parks) and Katie's Candy Company. Finally, if you are in the mood for a tattoo then Hart & Huntington Tattoo Company is the place for you!

Universal CityWalk Nightlife:

As far as bars and nightclubs are concerned, you will find Red Coconut Club, Pat O' Briens, CityWalk's Rising Star, the groove and Fat Tuesday. You will also find live music played at Hard Rock Live Orlando. Lone Palm Airport is also an outdoor bar just across from Jimmy Buffet's.

If you fancy partying the night away, then you may want to take advantage of the $11.99 *CityWalk* Party Pass (annual Passholders get 20% off for up to 4 people) which allows you unlimited one-night access to all of the following locations:

- CityWalk's Rising Star
- Jimmy Buffett's Margaritaville
- the groove
- Pat O'Brien's
- Red Coconut Club
- Bob Marley – A Tribute to Freedom

Note: A party pass will not allow you entry when special ticketed events are taking place in a nightclub.

If you do not own a Party Pass, the cover charge for a single nightclub is $7 and entertainment usually begins at 9:00pm. Hard Rock Café does not have a cover charge.

Top Tip: If you turn up before 9:00pm you will often be able to get in to these locations and not have to pay a cover charge.

If you would like to upgrade, for about $3 more you can get the *CityWalk* Party Pass + Movie ticket which allows you entry to all the aforementioned locations plus entry into one movie on the same day! This can be purchased at Guest Services.

Multi-day tickets and Flextickets include a free Party Pass that is valid for 14 days from first admission to the parks. So, multi-day ticket holders will not need to spend any extra to enjoy the nightlife. Blue Man Show ticket holders can also use their ticket stub for free CityWalk club access.

Chapter 8

For the little ones:

It is hard to imagine Universal Orlando as being a place for small kids when you have rides such as *The Incredible Hulk Coaster* and *Dr. Doom's Fear Fall* dominating the skyline. It is by no means anything like the Disney theme parks a few miles down the road, but Universal has not completely forgotten about the smallest members of the family. Both theme parks have areas dedicated especially to children.

We recommend you measure your child before leaving for Universal Orlando Resort, this means that you will be able to know in advance how tall your child is and avoid them getting excited about attractions they cannot ride. There is nothing more disappointing than being slightly too short for a ride they have waited to do for months – ride operators will not bend the rules, even for half an inch, for everyone's safety. Chapter 12 features a section with the minimum height requirements for all attractions that have them.

On the other hand, do remember that every kid has a different comfort zone, and some may well be frightened of an attraction even if they meet the minimum height requirements. Gently prompting and encouraging them is fine; forcing them to ride is not.

Important: Unlike at the Walt Disney World Resort, baby formula and diapers are not sold at the Universal parks.

Universal Studios Florida:

The small members of the family will enjoy seeing Gru and the gang at *Despicable Me: Minion Mayhem* (40 inches/1.02m minimum height) in a 3D simulator ride. *E.T. Adventure* (34 inches/0.87m minimum height) can be a little dark but is a relaxing ride – note that some kids may not enjoy the sensation of flying. *Woody Woodpecker's Nuthouse Coaster* (36 inches/0.92m minimum height) is a gentle rollercoaster for starters. The surrounding play areas in *Woody Woodpecker's KidZone* are great fun for kids, such as the nearby *Curious George Goes To Town* play area.

For entertainment, kids are sure to love *A Day in the Park with Barney* - a live interactive stage show featuring the dinosaur himself, and the *Universal Superstar parade* where they can see all their favorite characters.

The Simpsons Ride (40 inches/1.02m minimum height) also features great characters (note this may be scary due to the immersion through the huge screen and simulator).

Islands of Adventure:

In *Islands of Adventure* kids will be sure to love the *Seuss Landing* area of the park with its bright colors, play areas and meet and greets, as well as several rides which are suitable for all ages including the *Caro-Seuss-el; One Fish, two Fish, Red Fish, Blue Fish* (Children under 48 inches/1.22m must ride with an adult); and *The High in the Sky Seuss Trolley Train Ride* (40 inches/1.02m minimum to ride accompanied by an adult, or 48 inches/1.22m to ride alone).

In the *Toon Lagoon* area, you will also find several water play areas for kids (or adults) to splash around in. *Marvel Super Hero Island* also features *Storm Force Accelatron* (An adult must accompany those under 48 inches/1.22m), which essentially is just a themed teacup ride.

The *Jurassic Park Discovery Centre* can also be a fun, and educational, place to take kids to learn about dinosaurs.

Once the kids get a little older but are not yet ready to brave the likes of *The Hulk* you can visit *Pteranodon Flyers* (36 inches/0.92m minimum height), *Flight of the Hippogriff* (36 inches/0.92m minimum height) and *The Amazing Adventures of Spider-Man* (40 inches/1.92m minimum height).

Chapter 9

Services:

Photo Connect Star Card Package:

On-ride and in-park photos are expensive souvenirs, after all they are just a bit of ink on paper. No one really wants to pay $20 or $30 for a single photo, no matter how good the quality is. Now, Universal Orlando Resort has the perfect solution with the *Photo Connect Star Card*. If you are familiar with Disney's PhotoPass system, this functions quite similarly (but with less in-park photographers and a more affordable price).

The Star Card package is a physical card on a lanyard which you scan any time you have your photo taken – all these photos are automatically uploaded to the Photo Connect website where you can later download them at full resolution. You will receive two cards with your Star Card package, meaning a group can split up and get ride photos at the same time on one account.

Photo Connect includes on-ride photos, character photos and in-park photographer photos on the same card!

The best way to get a *Photo Connect Star Card* is either to visit the Photo Connect stores located at the entrance to each park – these are clearly signposted. Alternatively, after you have ridden your first attraction that features an on-ride photo, you can also visit the ride's photo purchasing location and ask to purchase the *Star Card package*.

You can use your Star Card at the following locations:

Universal Studios Florida Locations:
- On Location (Park Entrance Photos)
- E.T.'s Toy Closet & Photo Spot
- SpongeBob SquarePants Meet and Greet
- MEN IN BLACK Alien Attack
- Harry Potter and the Escape from Gringotts
- Shutterbutton's Photography Studio (with the ShutterButton's package)
- Revenge of the Mummy
- Hollywood Rip Ride Rockit
- Donkey Photo Op (near Shrek 4-D)
- TRANSFORMERS In-Queue Photo Op
- The Simpsons Photo Op
- Roaming Universal Studios Florida characters where applicable
- Despicable Me Super Silly Stuff Store Photo Op

Universal's Islands of Adventure Locations:
- DeFotos Expedition Photography (Park Entrance Photos)
- Spider-Man Photo Op in Marvel Alterniverse Store
- In-Queue Photo Op at The Amazing Adventures of Spider-Man
- The Incredible Hulk Coaster
- Dudley Do-Right's Ripsaw Falls
- Jurassic Park River Adventure
- T-Rex Automated Photo Capture in Jurassic Park
- Harry Potter and the Forbidden Journey
- The High In The Sky Seuss Trolley Train Ride! In-Queue Photo Op
- Roaming Islands of Adventure Characters where available
- The Grinch™ Seasonal Photo Op

There are a few different *Star Card* packages you can get. The one you choose will depend on how long you will be visiting:
- One day – $69.99 plus tax online, not available in-park
- Three consecutive days – $89.99 plus tax online, and $99.99 plus tax in-park
- Fourteen consecutive days – $139.99 plus tax online, not available in-park
- Shutterbutton's Star Card Package – $139.99 plus tax online

For most visitors, the three-day package offers the best value.

As well as the digital downloads of the photos, the price of the Star Card Package also includes: access to the 'Amazing Pictures' app which allows you to view your photos on your iOS or Android smartphone; and discounts on in-park ride photo prints.

The three-day package also includes these additional benefits: 1 free 5x7 or 8x10 print in a folder; 1 free 4x6 print; $5.00 5x7 or $10.00 8x10 prints at participating Photo Connect locations; and $2.00 4x6 prints at participating Photo Connect locations.

The Shutterbutton's Star Card Package includes unlimited Digital Downloads for 3 consecutive days; one 5x7 print; one 4x6 Print, and a Shutterbutton's DVD.

Annual pass holders can pay $139.99 plus tax and have unlimited photos for the duration of their pass. In-park this will cost $10 more. This can quickly pay for itself after a few visits!

One unadvertised feature of the Star Card is that you can add unlimited photos from Wet n' Wild water park to your account for $20 when you arrive at the water park. Make sure to keep your Star Card with you at all times.

Top Tip: You can save $10 on select Star Card packages by buying before you go at **https://presale.amazingpictures.com/PhotoConnect.aspx**. Remember that certain options such as the 1-day package are also exclusive to online pre-order.

As well as the Star Card packages, which are the best value option, you can also simply go up to any photographer and get an in-park photo. This will be added to a Photo Connect card that you can then use throughout the day at both theme parks. Before the end of the day visit one of the Photo Connect stores where you can choose the best pictures and have them printed. You will need a new Photo Connect card for each day of your vacation, unless you purchase the Star Card package. All in-park photos will be deleted at the end of the operating day.

Although superficially the system seems to be fairly similar to Disney's Photopass system, there are nowhere near as many in-park photographers (though the selection of on-ride photos is impressive).

Ride Lockers:

Many of the rides at Universal do not allow you to take your belongings onto them with you; instead any loose articles must be placed in free lockers. Here is how they work:
- You approach a locker station, these are located by the entrance to any ride that requires their use;
- Select 'Rent a locker' from the touch screen;
- Put your fingerprint on the reader and you will be assigned a locker

to put your stuff in;

- Go to the locker, put your belongings inside and press the green button next to the locker to lock the door. It is very important that you do this to make sure the locker is actually locked! If you forget to press the green button, the locker will automatically lock 5 seconds after the door is closed.

The lockers will be free for a certain period of time – this is always longer than the current posted attraction wait time. For example, a 90-minute queue for *The* Hulk would typically allow you 120 or 150 minutes of locker rental time to allow you to queue, experience the ride and collect your belongings without having to worry.

If you keep your stuff in the lockers longer than the free period, charges apply – the charge is $3 for each additional 30 minutes, up to a maximum daily charge of $20.

Lockers for the water rides are unusually not free and are priced at $4 for a set period of time (the wait time plus a margin), and $3 for each additional 30 minutes, up to a maximum daily charge of $20.

Top tip 1: If you rent a locker and your free time has expired because the line took longer than expected, tell a Team Member who will sort out the issue.
Top tip 2: If you forget your locker number, there is a feature on the locker terminals that will help you find it.
Top tip 3: Lockers for water rides are not free. In this case you can simply walk to a locker for another ride where they are free. This can save you a decent amount of money over the course of a trip. *Forbidden Journey* often has long locker rental times for example.
Top tip 4: The touchscreens on these lockers are very unresponsive, meaning that it can be hard for the touchscreen to register your finger touches. We recommend using your fingernails or your knuckles to touch the screen to solve this problem.

All-day park locker rentals:
Non-ride specific lockers are located by the entrance to each park – the cost is $8 per day for a standard locker or $10 per day for a family size locker. Guests may access these lockers as many times as they want throughout the day, though their location can be a pain, as they are not centrally located.

Universal Express Pass:

If you do not find waiting in line hugely enjoyable (and let's face it, who does?) and are willing to pay to get on rides quicker, then Universal's Express Pass system is perfect for you. The system is free for those staying on-site at the Hard Rock Hotel, Portofino Bay Hotel and Royal Pacific Resort. Otherwise, as a stand-alone product, Express is priced between $40 and $150 per day per person.

Essentially, your Express Pass is a card that allows you to skip the regular lines at almost every attraction in both theme parks. You will be able to enter a separate queue line that will be significantly shorter than the regular queue and drastically reduce your wait times. For shows, you will be allowed entry before guests who do not have an Express Pass – usually 15 minutes before the show is due to begin.

Which rides are not included?

Express Passes are valid on all attractions at both theme parks, with the following exceptions: *Harry Potter and The Forbidden Journey, Ollivander's Wand Shop (Hogsmeade)* and *Pteranodon Flyers* in Universal's Islands of Adventure. At Universal Studios Florida, *Kang & Kodos' Twirl 'n' Hurl, Hogwarts Express (both stations), Ollivander's Wand Shop (Diagon Alley)* and *Harry Potter and The Escape from Gringotts* do not offer Express Pass access.

How do I use it?

When at an attraction, simply show your Express Pass to the Team Member at the ride entrance, they will scan it and you will be directed to a separate queue line from non-Express Pass guests. Typically waits will be 15 minutes or less for rides even on the busiest days – often they will be much less. The exception is *Despicable Me: Minion Mayhem*, which has a wait time that is often longer than 15 minutes in the Express Pass queue line due to its slow loading nature.

Be aware that because you will be in a different queue line to the main one, Express Pass guests may lose some of the storyline told in the queue. This is particularly evident on *Revenge of the Mummy, Transformers* and *Men in Black*.

There are three types of Express Pass:
- **Universal Express Pass:** This is available for purchase both in the parks and online in advance. It allows one ride per participating attraction.
- **Universal Express Unlimited:** This is available for purchase online and in the parks. It allows unlimited rides on each participating attraction.

- **Park-To-Park Ticket + Universal Express Unlimited**: This is available for purchase online or over the phone (407-224-7840) and includes a regular park admission ticket for both parks and Universal Express Unlimited access for each day's entry – these tickets are available in one-day or multiple day versions. The ticket will expire when all park admission days on the ticket are used or 14 days after first use, whichever is sooner.
- **On-site Hotel Universal Express Unlimited Pass:** This is a perk for on-site hotel guests from the aforementioned hotels. It is included for each member of a party staying in the hotel room for every day of their stay including through all of the check in day and all of their check out day. It allows unlimited rides on each attraction. A photo of each guest will be printed onto this pass.

Each member of your party will need their own Express Pass. If you are not using an "On-site Hotel Universal Express Unlimited Pass" or a "Park-To-Park Ticket + Universal Express Unlimited" you will need to purchase a separate Express Pass for each day of your trip. There is no such thing as a multi-day Express Pass. In addition, you will need to have an Express Pass for each member of your party.

The Big Secret: Slash the Price of Express Passes
We mentioned early that select on-site hotels get Unlimited Express Pass access included in their stay. This means that staying at one of these hotels (Hard Rock Hotel, Portofino Bay Hotel and Royal Pacific Resort) is the best option if you are sure you want the Express Passes for your stay. These are luxury hotel resorts with fantastic amenities, and are located right next door to the theme parks. The queue-cutting privileges are just an extra bonus!

To give you an idea of the kind of money you can save, take a look at this: One night at the Royal Pacific Resort during the busiest season (Holiday) for two adults is $404 including complimentary Hotel Unlimited Express Passes. Remember that your stay includes complimentary passes for your entire stay, including check-in and check-out days.

Buying the same Express Passes separately for these days costs $150 per person, per day.

So, by staying at the Royal Pacific Resort you will save just under $200 and get a deluxe hotel included in the price.

The price gets even better when more people stay in the same room – one night for 4 people at the Royal Pacific Resort during the holiday season costs $454. In this case, you would save $800 total on the cost of Express Passes. Even if you don't need the hotel room, it is cheaper to book one, check-in, get your Express Passes and leave straight away.

If you are a family of five, you can get roll-away beds at the on-site hotels for an additional $25 per night, once again reducing the price per person per day.

These savings aren't exclusive to the holiday season either. You can get them year-round. Let's look at the Value Season in late January: two adults will pay $244 for a one-night stay at the Royal Pacific Resort. The Express Passes cost $70 per person, per day. Here you will save $36 total. This isn't the saving of $200 like during the Holiday season, but remember that there is a luxury hotel room included in this price too! Four adults would pay $294 for a one-night stay, saving $266 on Express Passes.

Generally, stays longer than one-night become poorer value as these hotels do have expensive nightly rates. This is why to take full advantage of this secret, you should only stay on-site for one night. Two days is more than enough to see everything on offer with Express Pass access!

As you can see, the maths is simple – if you want Express Passes, stay on-site!

Do I *need* an Express Pass?

In our opinion, during extremely busy periods, getting an Express Pass is almost essential to your visit. It will make sure that you will not need to wait hours upon hours in line, especially if you are limited to a short visit. However, the Express Passes are expensive and will often double the price of your admission. Having said this, with careful planning and by following our touring plans you should be able to do all the rides you want each day.

If you are visiting for multiple days, you should be able to do all the attractions in three full days at the parks without an Express Pass, even during the busiest seasons. In this case an Express Pass is not a necessity but you may wish to consider getting one day of Express to begin with, and then repeating attractions at a more leisurely pace on your other days without an Express Pass.

If you will be visiting outside of the peak periods of school breaks and public holidays, then the chances are that an Express Pass will be a waste of money. Outside of peak periods you should not need to wait more than 30 minutes for most attractions.

If you want to do both parks in one day (at any time of the year) you will still need an Express Pass.

Finally, if you are going to get an Express Pass we recommend you get the 'Unlimited' version – there is no point in paying so much money to reduce your waits and then only being able to do this once per ride. If you enjoy a ride, getting the Unlimited version of the Express pass means that you can re-ride it again.

Ultimately, if you cannot afford it, do not purchase an Express Pass. The money you spend on it can usually be used to feed your family in the parks all day and get several souvenirs. You will not miss out by not getting an Express Pass if you invest the time to get up early and follow our touring plans – yes, you will wait longer in line than those who have Express Passes, but you will potentially save hundreds of dollars in the process too.

Top tip 1: We do not recommend buying Express Passes in advance, unless you know you want them *and* you know that the parks are going to be busy. If you are unsure, wait until you are inside the parks and have seen the wait times – this way you can make the decision there and then. There is no advanced purchase discount, so you won't lose out with this method.

Top tip 2: If you are buying your Express Park tickets at the parks, don't do it from the Express Pass kiosk outside the park gates – the queue line here is usually much longer than at the kiosks just inside the park.

Top tip 3: Holders of the top-tier annual pass get complimentary Express Pass access after 4:00pm.

Top Tip 4: During certain periods of the year there are after-4:00pm Express Passes on sale for only $36 – these are infinitely more valuable when the park is open later. You will need to ask for these specifically, as they will not be listed in advance.

Top Tip 5: The "Park-To-Park Ticket + Universal Express Unlimited" ticket bundle works out cheaper than purchasing park admission and Universal Express Unlimited access separately.

Top Tip 6: If you are staying on-site and get a free Hotel Express Pass, this only applies during regular park hours. During extra-hours events where a separate admission ticket is required, such as Halloween Horror Nights, you will need to purchase an event-specific Express Pass.

Single Rider:

One of the best ways to significantly reduce your time waiting in queue lines is to use the Single Rider queue instead of the regular queue line. This is a completely separate queue that is used to fill free spaces on ride vehicles. For example, if a ride vehicle can seat 8 people and a group of 4 turns up, and then a group of 3 takes the other seats, then a 'single rider' will fill the empty space on the ride vehicle.

This ultimately makes the wait times shorter for everyone in the park as all spaces on ride vehicles are filled – single riders typically get on much quicker, and the regular line moves marginally quicker as all those single riders aren't in it!

If the parks do get extremely busy then sometimes single rider lines can be closed - this happens when the wait in the single rider line is the same or greater than the regular line, thereby undermining its purpose. If the line is full and cannot accommodate more guests, it will also be temporarily closed. If the park is almost empty, then sometimes these lines do not operate either, as there is no need for them.

Some rides have hidden Single Rider lines which are not advertised - in this case simply ask the first attraction host you see (usually at the entrance to the attraction) if the Single Rider queue line is open. If it is, then they will direct you accordingly. One prime example of this is *The Incredible Hulk Coaster* that does not advertise its single rider line - you have to ask for it. The *Harry Potter and the Forbidden Journey* single rider line can also be easily missed if you do not ask for it at the entrance.

If you are travelling as part of a group, you can still use the Single Rider queue line – just be aware that you will ride separately, but you can still meet each other at the exit once the ride is over.

Single rider lines are available on: *The Incredible Hulk, The Amazing Adventures of Spiderman, Harry Potter and the Forbidden Journey, Jurassic Park River Adventure, Dr. Doom's Fearfall, Dudley Do-Right's Ripsaw Falls, Transformers: The Ride, Hollywood Rip Ride Rockit, Revenge of the Mummy, Harry Potter and the Escape from Gringotts,* and *Men in Black: Alien Attack.*

Child Swap:

When two adults visit Universal Orlando Resort with a kid who does not or cannot ride, there could be a problem – each adult would need to queue separately, as the other waits with the child, they would then swap. This would mean that they'd essentially wait twice for each attraction. However, at Universal Orlando this doesn't need to happen; they have a solution – Child Swap.

Simply go up to a Team Member at an attraction entrance and ask to use Child Swap. Each ride works a little differently, but generally one or more adults will go in the standard queue line while another adult is directed to a child swap waiting area. Once the first group has queued up and then ridden the attraction, they proceed to the Child Swap area. Here the first group will stay with the child, and the person who originally sat with the child gets to ride straight away, without having to wait in the queue line again. This procedure may vary from attraction to attraction – make sure you ask the Universal Team Member at each attraction entrance about the specific procedure.

Q-Bot Ride reservation system:

This ride reservation scheme is billed as a more affordable alternative to Express Pass. The Q-Bot system is available anywhere that Express Pass can be purchased and is valid on all Express Pass rides, but it cannot be used for shows. The system is managed on a portable key ring-style device called a Q-Bot, which you rent for the duration of the day. It allows you to make ride reservations – these are not instant access passes.

How it works:

Unlike the Express Pass, this system does not get you onto rides any faster; instead it allows you to virtually reserve a place in line. For example: The time is currently 14:00 and the line for *Revenge of the Mummy* is 40 minutes. You select *Revenge of the Mummy* on your Q-Bot and you will make a reservation – in this example that reservation will be for 14:40 (the current time plus the time you would have spent in line). At 14:40, you can return to the attraction and you will be allowed into the Express Pass line – this line will get you onto the ride fairly quickly but may take up to 15 minutes during busy periods of the year.

Do not cancel your reservation as you walk up to each attraction, the ride operator will validate your Q-Bot and then allow you access to the Express Pass queue. For rides where you must stow your belongings in lockers, go to the ride entrance first, the ride attendant will validate your Q-Bot and you will be given a slip of paper to return to the Express Pass queue with, after you have stowed your belongings (including the Q-Bot).

Whilst you are waiting for your reservation time, you can use the time to experience another attraction or show in the regular queue lines, go shopping, get something to eat, etc. Used efficiently, you can double the amount of rides you experience per day and will spend a lot less time waiting in queue lines. Our favorite way to use the Q-bots is to make a reservation for a ride and then use that time to watch a show – this way you don't feel like you are waiting at all, as you are entertained.

One great feature of the Q-Bot is that you can make your ride reservations on the device wherever you are in the park, without the need to be physically present at an attraction to reserve – this means, for example, that you could be having lunch and make a reservation for *Despicable Me Minion Mayhem*.

Cancelling reservations:

You may cancel reservations at any time on the device, but you may only have one active ride reservation at a time. In order to create another reservation, you must experience the ride or cancel a reservation. Going back to our previous example, you can ride *Revenge of the Mummy* any time after 14:40. If it is 14:40 or later and you have still not used your *RoTM* reservation, you cannot book another ride reservation until you ride *RoTM* or cancel the reservation.

If you cancel a reservation, it is the equivalent of you leaving the queue line – you lose your place, and if you later want to reserve for the same ride, you must wait the full wait time (as if you were joining the queue line once again from the start).

What are my options?

As with Express Pass, there are two versions of the – one provides one reservation per ride, the other provides unlimited reservations per ride so you can make multiple reservations for the same ride throughout the day.

of Express Passes and the Q-Bot and an unlimited supply
arse the Express Passes win, as you will be on a ride within a
minutes – and usually in less than 5 minutes. However, if you
hited budget and do not like waiting in long lines then this
erfect system for you.

Theoretically you will not need to queue at all for rides as you make
reservations, and use that time instead to watch shows, shop, dine and meet
characters. In reality though, the Q-Bot will usually allow you to double the
number of attractions you do as you use the normal queue line for one, and
make a reservation for another. To make the out of this system, we
recommend making Q-Bot reservations for the rides with the longest waits
rather than those with shorter waits.

If you are visiting both parks in one day, and want to skip the lines at both,
then the Q-Bot is unlikely to be a good option as you will need to purchase
one Q-Bot at each park which is a lot of hassle and becomes tiresome – we
recommend an Express Pass in this case, despite the extra cost.

Note 1: There is no two-park version of this system, it can only be purchased
for one park – if you want to use Q-Bot for a second park then you must rent
each Q-Bot separately.

Note 2: Q-Bot is not necessarily offered every day of the year. There are days
when only Express Passes are sold.

Note 3: When you purchase access to a Q-Bot you will receive a voucher that
will need to be exchanged elsewhere inside the park. There you will sign a
contract stating you will return the device, and provide credit or debit card
payment details. You cannot use the Q-Bot system without a credit or debit
card. If the Q-Bot is not returned or is damaged, then you will be charged a
$50 fee per Q-Bot.

Internet access:

Internet access has become indispensable over the past few years – whether
you need to send a business email, check the route to your next destination,
book a hotel room, check your credit card bill or upload a photo to
Instagram. Theme parks have started offering complimentary Wi-Fi access
over the past couple of years, and in 2014 this service finally reached the
Universal Orlando Resort.

You can find free Wi-Fi throughout both theme parks and the City to connect to. The network is called "Universal". Xfinity cable cus simply login with their account credentials. Non-Xfinity customer access to free Wi-Fi upon providing their zip code and email add: US users can just use a random five-digit number such as 32820.

In-room Wi-Fi access is offered at no cost to hotel guests for the "standard" level – if you require higher speed access there is a "premium" option available for $15 per day. The lobby and pool areas in all the on-site hotels have free Wi-Fi that you can access regardless of whether or not you are staying at the hotel.

The Universal Orlando app:

'The Official Universal Orlando Resort App' available for free on smartphones allows you to access wait times for all attractions when inside the parks, get directions to attractions with a step-by-step visual representation, see upcoming show times and special events, be alerted when a wait time drops below a certain number, see park and resort maps, find guest amenities, see park hours, set show time alerts, share on social media, and locate food items.

Universal Orlando is also promising that in future it will add new features such as instant Express Pass purchase (even in queue lines!) and customizable itineraries to be made. The App is available for free on the Apple App Store and the Google Play store.

Package delivery:

One great service that many theme parks offer to their guests is package delivery and Universal Orlando is no exception. This service allows you to purchase an item and then have it stored until later in the day when you can pick it up, without having to carry it around with you all day. The two places you can have your package sent to are:

- **The front of the park** – By each of the theme parks' exit turnstiles you will see a small shop that is accessible both from inside and outside the park. Purchases you have made throughout the day will be sent here for you to pick up later. Please allow up to 4 hours for delivery to this window.
- **Your hotel room** – You can also have the package delivered straight to your hotel room if you are staying at one of the on-site Universal hotels. The only caveat is that it will be delivered the next day between 9:00am and 4:00pm. Therefore, this service is unavailable the day before checkout or the day of checkout itself so it is really

only suitable for stays of 3 nights or longer.

Stroller and Wheelchair Rental:

Both theme parks offer stroller and wheelchair rentals, as well as the rental of motorized ECVs. The rental area is located to the left hand side of each park's turnstiles.

You can rent the following:
*Single Stroller – $15 per day
*Single Kiddie Car – $18 per day
*Double Stroller – $25 per day
*Double Kiddie Car – $28 per day
*Wheelchairs – $12 per day, plus a $50 deposit.
*ECVs – $50 per day, plus a $50 deposit.

The strollers are just standard strollers. The kiddie car is a stroller that is designed to look like a car with an enclosed front foot area, making it harder for kids to slip out, and a steering wheel for kids to play with.

ECVs must be operated by a single person aged 18 years old or over. Wheelchairs can also be rented in the parking rotunda area.

Chapter 10

Guests with disabilities:

Visiting a theme park can seem like a complicated process for someone with a disability, but Universal Orlando has worked hard to make your experience as positive as possible and to give you as much of the full theme park experience as they can. Although, we could not possibly cover every kind of disability in this section we have tried to include as much information as possible.

Universal Attraction Assistance Pass:

A Universal Attraction Assistance Pass can really ease the day for some visitors. In order to obtain it you will need to go to Guest Services (to the right through the turnstiles) and ask for the Attraction Assistance Pass.

Although it is not required, we strongly recommend you get a note from your doctor in English explaining what exactly you need help with - whether it is not waiting in the sun or not waiting for prolonged periods of time in line or not waiting in crowded areas. It will all depend on your situation. Your doctor does NOT need to explain what your disability is, merely what help you require in the theme parks.

The Universal Team Members at Guest Services will ask you several question to determine eligibility and what type of help you will need – as mentioned before, a letter from a doctor is not required but will greatly assist this process. You will then be issued an Attraction Assistance Pass and it will be explained to you.

Using the pass:

When you reach an attraction you would like to experience, show your Assistance Pass to the first Team Member you see at the entrance of the line (this person is called the attraction 'greeter').

If the regular attraction wait time is less than 30 minutes, then you will be immediately directed towards an alternative queue - this is often the Express Pass queue line.

If the regular wait time for the attraction is more than 30 minutes then the greeter will write down a time on your Pass to return – we will call this a 'reservation' for the purpose of this guide. When that time comes around, show your pass with the reservation time at the ride entrance and you will be allowed entry through the alternative queue. Remember that this is NOT a front-of-the-line ticket and waits can still be up to 15 minutes.

You can only hold one ride 'reservation' at any one time. You may still enjoy accelerated entrance to attractions with less than a 30-minute wait, even if you have an active reservation. If you want to change which attraction you have a reservation for simply go to the next attraction and make a reservation with the attraction's greeter at the entrance - this will automatically void your previous reservation. An Assistance Pass allows up to 25 reservations, which should be more than enough for a single day.

The Assistance Pass will be valid for up to 6 people in the person's party.

Express Guest Assistance Pass:
The Express Guest Assistance Pass is used in situations where waiting in any form of long queue or having to return later is simply not possible and therefore the classic Universal Attractions Assistance Pass is not suitable. As such, this pass is aimed at a much more limited number of guests and it is more difficult to obtain. This Pass does not require proof with a doctor's note, but a note can really help in this situation. You may need to ask to speak to a manager to obtain this card.

Generally speaking, the Express Guest Assistance Pass is for guests with certain mental health disorders, though a full list is not disclosed.

This Pass will allow you to enter the alternative queue instantly without the need to obtain a return time, no matter what the wait time is. This is NOT a front-of-the-line ticket and you must wait in the alternative queue.

The Express GAP is not valid at *Harry Potter and the Escape from Gringotts* and the *Hogwarts Express* at Universal Studios Florida. It is also not valid at *Harry Potter and the Forbidden Journey, the Hogwarts Express, and Pteranodon Flyers* at Islands of Adventure. If you wish to visit the above rides, then a classic Attraction Assistance Pass will be needed, or you will need to use the regular queue line instead. Overall, this Pass acts very similarly to the Universal Express Pass Unlimited.

Other accommodations for disabled guests:
Deaf/Hard of Hearing – For guests who are deaf or hard of hearing, many in-park shows have interpreted performances. The timings of these are printed on the park map. Closed captioning and assistive listening devices, guidebooks for guests with disabilities, and attraction scripts are also available at Guest Services in each theme park.

Mobility Impairment and wheelchairs – The whole of Universal Orlando has been designed to be as wheelchair-accessible as possible with ramps instead of steps. All shopping and dining facilities are accessible. Guests who would like to use a stroller as a wheelchair should ask for a special tag from Guest Services.

Outdoor stage shows also have designated areas for wheelchair users and their parties. Rides are accessible – some will require a transfer; others will allow you to ride in your wheelchair.

You can get a wheelchair at the parking rotunda to help with the considerable distance from the rotunda to the theme parks if necessary – simply ask the Team Members here. Alternatively, you can rent these inside the theme parks. Guests may pay the additional cost for an ECV once at the theme park or continue to use the wheelchair throughout the day.

Note that you do not NEED to have an Attraction Assistance Pass if you are in a wheelchair as all rides have an accessible entrance, but it can make things easier when there are particularly long queues, so we do recommend it. If you, or someone you are with, suffers from a disability that is not easily seen we thoroughly recommend the use of one of the Assistance Passes – without one you will need to use the regular queue line.

Service Animals are permitted throughout the theme parks but each attraction will have a specific way of boarding. Kennels exist at some attractions for service animals. The greeters at the entry of each attraction will be able to provide more information.

Rides and shows:
Special restrictions apply to guests with prosthetic limbs and guests with oxygen tanks. More information about rides and shows specifically is available through the Riders Guide for Rider Safety & Guests with Disabilities (PDF file). It can be downloaded online from **http://www.universalorlando.com/Images/Riders_Guide_tcm13-26195.pdf**

Chapter 11

Dining:

When visiting the Universal Orlando Resort you will find an abundance of food choices, from standard theme park fare to fine dining. Eating somewhere you have never visited can be daunting, especially for picky eaters, so this chapter aims to help.

At Universal you are able to walk into quick-service (fast-food style) places and get food within a few minutes, get food and drinks from snack carts throughout the parks or opt for a full sit down meal. You can even eat at one of the character dining locations where characters come round to each table and pose for photos.

For those wishing to plan their meal budget in advance, Universal offers programs to help: the dining plans.

Quick Service Universal Dining Plan

The Quick Service Universal Dining Plan is available to all guests and can be bought at the theme parks at any Quick Service location, online at **UniversalOrlando.com** or at dining reservation kiosks in the parks. It is accepted at over 100 locations at the Universal Orlando Resort.

The cost of the quick service dining plan is $19.99 + tax for adults and $12.99 + tax per child.

Each day purchased on the Universal Quick Service Dining Plan entitles you to:

- 1 Quick Service meal – with Entree and Non-alcoholic beverage. 1 Snack – From food carts or quick service locations such as popcorn, ice cream or a frozen beverage.
- 1 Non-Alcoholic Beverage – From food carts or quick service locations.

Guests who purchase the Quick Service Dining Plan in advance must pick up their dining plan card with their credits to use the scheme. You will receive a voucher when you book your dining plan that can be exchanged in the theme parks or *CityWalk*. The voucher can be exchanged for a card at the Ticket Centre or Guest Services at either theme park, or the Dining Reservation Cart at either theme park or *CityWalk*.

The Quick Service Dining Plan can be redeemed at all food locations owned and operated by Universal Orlando in Universal Studios Florida and Islands of Adventure, and at select *CityWalk* locations including Hot Dog Hall of Fame and Bread Box.

In our opinion the quick service plan is not going to be a great purchase if you are looking for value for money, as you would really have to try hard to profit from this dining plan and you would need to eat the most expensive entrees on the menu.
Plus, this isn't what we would classify as a dining plan, as there is only one actual meal included – the rest are drinks and snacks. This may not be enough for some people.

If, however, you want to have meals paid for in advance then you may enjoy this option. If you are using one of the refillable drink options discussed later in this chapter you are guaranteed to lose money with the Quick Service Dining Plan, as refills are so cheap.

Top Tip: You can add a Coca-Cola Freestyle cup to this plan for only $6 extra per day. More on these cups later in this chapter.

Universal Dining Plan

Unlike the Quick Service Universal Dining Plan, the Universal Dining Plan is only available to guests who have booked a vacation package through Universal Parks & Resorts Vacation or an authorized reseller – this includes both on-site and off-site hotels. The Dining Plan cannot be purchased in the parks in any form.

The cost of the dining plan is $51.99 + tax for adults and $17.99 for children (Ages 3 to 9).

Each day purchased on the Dining Plan entitles you to:
- 1 Table Service meal – with Entree, Dining Plan Dessert and Non-alcoholic beverage.
- 1 Quick service meal – with Entree and Non-alcoholic beverage.
- 1 Snack – From food carts or quick service locations such as popcorn, ice cream or a frozen beverage.
- 1 Beverage – From food carts or quick service locations.

For those familiar with the Disney Dining Plan at Walt Disney World this is very similar in nature but there is one crucial difference: whereas at Disney you have to purchase a Dining plan for the entire stay, (e.g. At Disney an 8-day stay would mean you would have to purchase 8 days of dining plan), at Universal you buy however many days' worth of credits you need. So it would be possible to purchase 3 days' worth of food during an 8-day stay. You must purchase the plan for every member of your family aged over two years old.

Furthermore, you do not need to use all your credits in 3 days, or even 3 consecutive days. For example, with a 3-day dining package you would get 3 table service meal credits, 3 quick service meal credits, 3 snack credits and 3 beverage credits. With the Universal Dining Plan, you could split these between several days throughout the entire duration of your stay. You could have a table service meal one day and a snack, and then two quick service meals another day - the credits are available for your entire stay.

For character fans, you can use one full service credit for the Superstar Character Breakfast at Cafe La Bamba.

The Universal Dining Plan can be redeemed at most food locations owned and operated by Universal Orlando in Universal Studios Florida and Islands of Adventure, and at select *CityWalk* locations including Antojitos, Margaritaville and Red Oven Pizza Bakery. No on-site hotel restaurants are part of this dining plan.

Guests who purchase the Dining Plan must pick up their dining plan card with their credits to use the scheme. You will receive a voucher when you book your vacation to be exchanged in the theme parks or *CityWalk*. The voucher can be exchanged for a card at the Ticket Centre Desk or Guest Services at either theme park, or Dining Reservation Carts at either theme park or *CityWalk*. It can also be picked up at on-site hotels.

For an upcharge of $20 per adult or $7 per child you can use one of your credits for the Cinematic Spectacular Dining Experience at Lombard's Seafood Grille.

Our opinion: The Dining Plan is a good option for food lovers, but compared to Disney's system the dining plan still has a few niggles to work out. The system was only introduced in 2013 at Universal, though, so it's understandable. Firstly, exchanging a voucher given at booking for a card is annoying and time consuming.

Secondly, eating locations in *CityWalk* are still limited on the plan (though they have expanded over time) – all the other restaurants are inside the theme parks, so you will need park admission each day to make the most of the plan. Frustratingly, as the on-site hotels are operated by Loews and not Universal, no on-site hotel restaurants are included in the plan.

Thirdly, each card is assigned its own credits and operates independently. As such a parent wanting to get four ice creams needs to have all four cards with them, and each ice cream would be processed separately. The credits are not grouped between cards like the Disney Dining Plan. This can be very time consuming.

Having mentioned all these caveats, it is a good system. If you like having all your meals pre-paid with one less expense to worry about, and like eating table service meals, then this is the perfect plan for you. In addition, this plan does generally offer better value than the Quick Service dining plan, especially if you eat the most expensive items on the menus, meaning that you can often end up saving money here.

Note: Gratuities are not included in the price of the Dining Plan.

List of all Universal Dining Plan locations:

Universal Studios Florida:
Beverly Hills Boulangerie – Quick Service location.
Fast Food Boulevard – Quick Service location.
Finnegan's Bar and Grill – Table Service location.
KidZone Pizza Company – Quick Service location.
Leaky Cauldron – Quick Service location.
Lombard's Seafood Grille – Table Service location.
London Taxi Hut – Quick Service location.
Louie's Italian Restaurant – Quick Service location.
Mel's Drive In – Quick Service location.
Richter's Burger Co. – Quick Service location.
San Francisco Pastry Company – Sandwiches and Pastries location.
Superstar Character Breakfast at Café La Bamba – Character dining.
Universal Studios' Classic Monsters Café – Quick Service location.

Islands of Adventure:
Blondie's – Quick Service location.
Cafe 4 – Quick Service location.
Captain America Diner – Quick Service location.

Circus McGurks Cafe Stoo-pendous – Quick Service location.
Comic Strip Cafe – Quick Service location.
Confisco Grill and Backwater Bar – Table service location.
Croissant Moon Bakery – Quick service location.
Fire Eater's Grill – Quick Service location.
Green Eggs and Ham Café – Quick Service location.
Mythos Restaurant – Table Service location.
The Burger Digs – Quick Service location.
The Grinch & Friends Character Breakfast (Seasonal) – Character dining.
Three Broomsticks – Quick Service location.
Thunder Falls Terrace – Quick Service location.
Wimpy's – Quick Service location.

<u>CityWalk:</u>
Auntie Anne's Pretzels – Snack location.
Antojitos Authentic Mexican Food – Table service location.
Bob Marley – A Tribute to Freedom – Table service location.
Blue Man Group Theater Coke – Snack location.
Bread Box Hand Crafted Sandwiches – Quick Service location.
Cold Stone Creamery – Snack location.
Cinnabon – Quick service location. Dining Plan for selected snacks.
Hot Dog Hall of Fame – Quick Service location.
Icon Hub Cart – Snack location.
Jimmy Buffet's Margaritaville – Table service location.
Menchie's Frozen Yogurt – Quick Service location.
NBA City – Table service location.
Pat O' Brien's – Table service location.
Red Oven Pizza Bakery – Quick Service location.
Starbucks Coffee – Accepts Universal Dining Plan for selected snacks and beverages only.
The Cowfish – Table service location.
Vivo Italian Kitchen – Table service location.

Refillable Cups, Coca Cola Freestyle and Popcorn Buckets

There are two options for refillable drinks in the theme parks: the classic refillable cups and the Coca Cola Freestyle refillable cups.

A refillable cup costs $8.99 plus tax. Once you have purchased the cup you are then eligible for discounted refills priced at 99 cents plus tax. The cups can be refilled virtually everywhere within the two theme parks that serves fountain drinks – that is pretty much every quick-service and full-service location, but not food carts. You can also have your cup refilled in *CityWalk*, but not at any of the on-site hotels. Once you have purchased one of these cups you can get unlimited 99-cent refills for life under the current policy. Note that refills are for fountain drinks only such as Coca Cola, Fanta and Sprite. You will not be able to get discounted refills on any specialty drinks such as Butterbeer or any specialty drinks from Simpsons' Fast Food Blvd.

You can also get discounts on refills of tea, lemonade, and cider inside the Wizarding World of Harry Potter, and on slushies and ICEEs elsewhere at the parks.

Refillable popcorn buckets work in the same way as the refillable cups listed above – you pay $5.99 for the popcorn bucket, and then refills are $1.29 plus tax each. There are four places at each theme park where your souvenir bucket can be refilled: just look for the big popcorn machines – these are usually outdoors. There are no popcorn refills at *CityWalk*, nor at any of the on-site hotels. Popcorn refills are only available for standard popcorn; flavored popcorn is not available at a discount and must be purchased at full price.

Finally, there are the Coca Cola Freestyle machines that operate in a completely different manner to the two schemes above. You pay $12.99 plus tax for a Coca Cola Freestyle cup. You then visit any of the 8 Coca Cola Freestyle locations - 4 in each park (all in quick-service restaurants, bar one in *Islands of Adventure*) and refill your cup for free for that day – there are also other Freestyle machines throughout the parks that are not inside quick service locations.

The cup has an RFID chip and will only be activated for that day. After that, the cup will not work for free refills. There are over 100 different Coke drink mixes you can choose from at the machine, or you can stick to the plain old Coke products – it is up to you. As you must wait ten minutes between refills with Coca Cola Freestyle, this discourages sharing. Additional days can be added at $5.99 a day. There are no Coke Freestyle stations at *CityWalk* or any of Universal's on-site hotels that can be used with this system.

Dining reservations:

Dining at Universal Orlando Resort is varied, with options ranging from quick service meals to full-blown table service locations. When you want to sit down and have a meal in a busy theme park, you do not want to be kept waiting and you want to make sure there is a seat reserved for you. That is where dining reservations come in.

Unlike some of the other theme parks in the area (such as those operated by a mouse), at Universal you will not have trouble making dining reservations. There is no need to sit by your computer 180 days before you want your meal either. Instead, it is simple – you can browse through the various restaurants and their menus on the Universal Orlando website, and book your table via OpenTable whenever you want at no cost to you.

With the exception of very busy seasons, you should be able to get a reservation for most restaurants even 4 or 5 days in advance. If there is a specific place you want to eat we recommend you book your table as early as possible. However, we have frequently decided that we would like to eat a particular location and have known to get reservations on the very same day.

If you do want to book in advance, then the official Universal website is the place to go. You will need to visit **https://www.universalorlando.com/Restaurants/50-Great-Restaurants.aspx**. We do not recommend going directly to the OpenTable website as it is difficult to navigate and you cannot find all the restaurants at the Resort on one page.

Top 5 Table Service restaurants at Universal Orlando:

Universal has Table Service restaurants dotted across its theme parks, *CityWalk* and the resort hotels, so finding the best one can be a bit of a task. Luckily, we have rounded up those that you really should not miss out on below. Note that prices and menus change all the time with seasons and chefs - those which we have listed were correct as of when we ate at the locations and should merely be taken as examples.

1. Mythos *(Islands of Adventure)* – Mythos is often rated the number one theme park restaurant in all of Orlando, let alone just Universal Orlando. Mythos is a pure delight to eat in, with its lavish interior, exotic menu and, perhaps surprisingly, rather fair prices. Mythos will truly transport you to a different world. Entrees are priced between $10 and $20. The food ranges from sandwiches to Shortribs, Asian Salmon and Mahi Mahi. Note: Mythos is often only open for lunch.

2. Finnegan's Bar and Grill *(Universal Studios Florida)* – Finnegan's is always a fun place to dine in, or to simply go in for a quick drink. Themed as an Irish Pub, there is a lot of fun to be had as well as some delightful treats. Entrees are priced between $10 and $22. The food ranges from sandwiches to Fish 'n' Chips, Beef Stew and Sirloin Steak.

3. Confisco Grille & Backwater bar *(Islands of Adventure)* – Located in the *Port of Entry* park entrance area, Confisco Grille has a more traditional range of theme park food which may be better for families with younger children who are not quite ready to eat the Mahi Mahi at Mythos. It is also a more relaxed atmosphere. Entrees are priced between $9 and $18. You will find wood-oven pizzas, sandwiches, pasta and fajitas to name just a few of the items on the menu.

4. NBA City *(CityWalk)* – Many ignore this restaurant when walking past, perhaps discounting it as tacky because of its basketball theme. Do not be one of the people that makes that mistake; NBA City has some great food on offer and the portions are huge! The desserts in particular are to die for – try the Cinnamon Berries and the fried Cheesecake for an unforgettable end to a meal. Entrees are priced between $10 and $34. There is a wide selection of food on offer from chicken quesadillas to pizzas, jambalaya, shrimp, salmon, pasta, and much more.

5. Emeril's *(CityWalk)* – Emeril's is the most premium of the Table Service dining experiences we have listed here, with prices to match. With New Orleans-inspired dishes, you can enjoy seeing your food be prepared in the open kitchen. Alternatively, indulge and book yourself into the Chef's private tasting room with space for ten people. Entrees are priced between $12 and $18 for lunch, and $24 to $30 for dinner. You will find food ranging from a soup of the day to shrimps and grits, calamari, lasagna and the 18-oz ultimate rib-eye steak.

Top 5 Quick Service restaurants at Universal Orlando:

Sometimes you do not necessarily want to sit down and have a three-course meal. You may want to use that time to watch a show, walk around the parks or ride your favorite attraction again – but that does not mean you want to compromise on taste. Here's out list of our favorite on-site quick service restaurants. Note that prices and entrees change often – those listed were correct as of the last time we ate at the locations and should merely be taken as examples.

1. Three Broomsticks *(Islands of Adventure)* – Everything about this restaurant puts it top of the pile of quick service locations: the atmosphere, the food and its opening hours. Three Broomsticks is open for all three meals: breakfast, lunch and dinner, and is the only restaurant inside *The Wizarding World of Harry Potter - Hogsmeade.* Entrees are priced between $8 and $15. Breakfast entrees include breakfasts from around the world: English, American and Continental Europe just to name a few. Lunch and dinner fare revolves around British dishes with some American classics available too. You will find Cornish pasties, fish & chips, shepherd's pie, as well as smoked turkey legs, rotisserie smoked chicken and spareribs.

2. Thunder Falls Terrace *(Islands of Adventure)* – This is another restaurant where the atmosphere really brings you into the story. Step foot into Thunder Falls and you are right in the middle of the world of Jurassic Park - and you get a spectacular view of the River Adventure ride splashdown from the wall of glass diving the restaurant and the Jurassic world outside. Entrees are priced between $9 and $16. You will find cheeseburgers on sale, as well as ribs, smoked turkey legs, wraps, as well as rotisserie chicken. The portion sizes are large at this restaurant. The rotisserie chicken has been dry every time we have eaten there so we cannot recommend that particular item, but the ribs are much better!

3. Louie's Italian Restaurant *(Universal Studios Florida)* – As far as pizzas and pasta are concerned for inside the theme parks, Louie's does it best. Outside the parks **Red Oven Pizza Bakery** does pizza even better (another way of getting a quick honorable mention in this section). It should be noted that there is not a huge variety of food on offer at Louie's and it is not particularly healthy. Entrees are priced between $6 and $14. You can also order a full pizza pie to share for between $29 and $36. Food on offer includes spaghetti and meatballs, pizza and fettuccine alfredo. The meatballs are surprisingly good for a theme park quick service location, as are the pizzas.

4. Krusty Burger *(Universal Studios Florida)* – If you want the slimiest of burgers then this is *the* place to go. Designed to be exactly as "artery-clogging" as the burgers are in 'The Simpsons' cartoons, Krusty Burger will not win any awards for being exotic but this location hands down has the best-tasting burgers at Universal. Entrees are priced between $8 and $13 with fries included. As well as burgers, you will find barbecue rib sandwiches and hot dogs. The burgers are, however, an acquired taste – many people we know didn't like the taste of the meat.

5. Croissant Moon Bakery *(Islands of Adventure)* – The food at the Croissant Moon Bakery genuinely is really great-tasting and far from your standard theme park fare. However, the bakery is not somewhere where you would go for a full-blown lunch or dinner meal, but rather is where you might prefer to go for breakfast or a light snack. **Top Tip**: This location is not listed on the theme park map; you will find it in the *Port of Entry* area of the park. Entrees are priced between $2.50 and $10. This location serves continental breakfasts, sandwiches, Paninis and most importantly delicious cakes! If you fancy a branded coffee, this is the place to go too!

Honorable Mention: Leaky Cauldron *(Universal Studios Florida)* –This location has a great atmosphere inside, and like its other Wizarding World companion in this section, you can be sure to get some good British grub at this location including Banger's and Mash, Cottage Pie, Toad in the Hole, Fish and Chips and more. Entrees are priced at $9 to $20 here.

Butterbeer Top Tips:

Butterbeer is the Wizarding World's signature drink and can be found in regular ($4.99), hot ($4.99) or frozen ($5.99) flavors – we recommend the frozen variety. Souvenir mugs can be purchased for an upcharge of $9 – these are merely souvenir mugs and do not provide discounted refills on Butterbeer but do for most other drinks.

Top Tip 1: If you are thinking of getting a Butterbeer in Hogsmeade go to the *Hog's Head* to get it - the lines are usually much shorter than from the carts outside and it is a fantastic place to relax.

Top Tip 2: If you want a Butterbeer in Hogsmeade at the start of the day then you will want to get it from the cart by Hogwarts Castle and not the one in Hogsmeade village opposite Dragon Challenge. The lines will be much shorter.

Top Tip 3: In our opinion, even better than regular or frozen Butterbeer, is the new amazingly-tasty Butterbeer ice-cream that you can get from Florean Fortescue's Ice-Cream Parlour in Diagon Alley.

Chapter 12

Tips, Savings and More:

Money saving tips:

Bring food from home – Universal allows you to bring your own food into the parks, so why not do exactly that? Whether it is a bag of chocolates or a drink, you can purchase these items at a fraction of the price anywhere outside of Universal property. For drinks, why not put them in a cooling bag (hard-sided coolers are not allowed in the parks) and/or freeze them to drink throughout the day. Food should be fine in a backpack throughout the day. Glass containers and bottles are not permitted in the parks.

Bring rain gear – There is a high likelihood that at some point during your Universal Orlando theme park adventure you will get wet, whether that is on one of the water rides or play areas, or whether you get caught in one of the famous Floridian thunderstorms. Either way we recommend you bring some sort of rain protection from home - either a raincoat, a poncho or even an umbrella (be aware of lightning and umbrellas though). This saves you 1) from purchasing these items in the theme parks at very inflated prices, and 2) buying new clothes when you get soaked to replace what you already have. Another tip: Those big human dryers outside the water rides that you can pay $5 to go into are not very effective – do not waste your money.

Buy tickets in advance – Whatever you do, do not buy tickets at the gate – you will waste time and pay more than you need to. As you are reading this guide, we can safely assume that you will be doing some planning before you go, so there is no excuse not to buy your tickets in advance. You can do this over the phone, online at www.universalorlando.com or through a third party - either way you will save at least $20 per multi-day ticket by not purchasing them at the gate. What's more, if you purchase these tickets through the official Universal Orlando Resort website you will receive a coupon that you can exchange for a booklet with up to $150 in money-off coupons. In addition, certain countries will find that they can get special deals such as the UK where you can get a 14-day ticket for the price of a standard 2-day two-park ticket on the official Universal Orlando website.

You do not NEED an Express Pass – If you make sure to follow our touring plans you will be able to complete both Universal Parks in two days, so if you have two days then Express Pass simply is not needed: you can save up to $135 per person on Express Passes alone. If you want to do everything in one day, Express Passes are a must.

If you want Express Passes, then stay on-site – On site hotels are expensive but one little-known perk of staying on-site at a select hotels is the unlimited Express Passes for everyone staying in the room. The best bit is that you get Unlimited Express Passes for the entire duration of your stay, including both check in and check out days. One great way to make the most of this is to simply book a one-night stay at a Universal hotel. On your check-in day despite the fact your room will only be available from 3:00pm onwards you can actually check in at any time and leave your bags and receive your Express Passes – this means you can theoretically get there at 7:00am or 8:00am, check in and head straight to the parks. On your checkout day your Express Passes are valid until theme park closing, even after you check out. Note: Express Passes are not included in rooms at the Cabana Bay Beach Resort, only at the deluxe on-site hotels.

Stay off-site – If you do not want to pay the comparatively high prices to stay at the on-site hotels, then stay off-site. There are many hotels that are only just off Universal Orlando Resort property – a two to three-minute drive away, or 15-minute walk. These rooms can cost a fraction of the price of the on-site hotels. Plus, at the on-site hotels you will have to pay a nightly parking fee, which you may not have to do at many off-site locations.

Loyalty Cards – AAA members, American Express Card holders and UK-based AA members can all receive different discounts throughout the resort. The AAA/AA discount is usually 10% at restaurants though be sure to ask for it any time you pay for anything.

Ride photos – Universal are pretty strict on you not being allowed to take photos of the park monitors showing your on-ride photos. As such we recommend that if you are planning on buying ride photos, you should purchase the Universal Photo Connect Star Card – see this guide's Service chapter for more on this. It will pay for itself if you plan on buying just a few ride photos

Stay at a partner hotel – Stay at one of Universal Orlando's partner hotels and you will receive in-room coupons whether you have booked the room directly or not, and depending on who you book it with, you may get early park admission too.

Free lockers – Universal charges for lockers on water rides but not on any other rides. Would they know for example if you put your belongings in another ride's lockers which are free and then walked over to the water ride? Absolutely not. It is up to you to decide if you use this trick or not as it does involve walking back and forth.

If you will be doing this, be prepared to do a lot of walking to save a few dollars. Also be prepared to look around for the ride with the longest wait times to store your belongings in - both *Harry Potter and the Forbidden Journey* and *Harry Potter and the Escape from Gringotts* often have long wait times but also have very crowded locker areas.

Get a *CityWalk* coupon book – This is a completely free coupon book offering savings all across *CityWalk*. You can get it from the small kiosk near the elevator between the two floors of *CityWalk*. You can also get dining information here. Vouchers from here are generally for food and offers vary throughout the year.

How to spend less time queuing:

Park opening – Make sure you get to the theme park well before it officially opens. Ideally you should be at the gate 30 minutes or more before opening. Remember it will take some time to park your car and get to the theme parks too. Early morning is the quietest point of the day and in the first hour you can usually do two or three of the biggest rides, something that would take several hours during the day. The parks are almost always opened earlier than advertised, particularly during busy periods.

Use the single rider lines – If you do not mind riding separately from the rest of your party, take advantage of the Single Rider lines – see our chapter dedicated to these. They will reduce your time in queue lines significantly meaning you can experience more things per day, and are available at a surprisingly high number of major attractions.

Touring Plans – We have expertly crafted touring plans which tell you what order to do the attractions in; these are devised to let you see as much as possible whilst spending as little time as possible in queues. Use them.

Parades and Fireworks – If you have a desire to get on to rides and no desire to see parades or fireworks, then use the time the shows are on to visit the big rides, as crowds dwindle during these big events

Parades – As a follow up tip, do not ride attractions near the parade route immediately after the parade, they will be busier than usual.

The 59-minute rule – If Universal closes its parks at 9:00pm, at that time the queue lines (not the rides) will be closed. Anyone in the queue line at park closing time will be allowed to ride, no matter how long the line is. This means that if you have one final ride to do and it is getting to park closing time, make sure that you are in queue line before the park closes and you will still be able to ride. This rule may not apply if an attraction has an exceptionally long line which would cause it to keep running for hours after park closing – recently, notably, *Escape from Gringotts* has limited guest entry before the park officially closes.

Early Park Admission

How do you fancy being able to get into the theme parks before other guests? Benefit from much shorter queue lines at select attractions, and an emptier park, with Universal's Early Park Admission (EPA).

During most of the year, Universal Orlando Resort offers one-hour early entry to one of the two theme parks. This benefit is available to on-site hotel guests and guests who have booked a Universal Vacation Package. It is available for every day of their stay including their check-in and check-out days.

At Islands of Adventure you will be able to access *The Wizarding World of Harry Potter: Hogsmeade* including all attractions (except Hogwarts Express which opens when Universal Studios Florida starts its operating day). Unofficially, you may also find that one attraction within *Seuss Landing* may also be operating – most of the time this is *The Cat in the Hat*, but this is subject to change.

At Universal Studios Florida, you will be able to access *The Wizarding World of Harry Potter: Diagon Alley* and its attractions, minus the Hogwarts Express which opens at the same time as Universal's Islands of Adventure.

Early entry is offered every day of the year for those staying at on-site hotels. It is also offered with vacation packages booked through Universal whether staying on-site or not, as long as you have booked through Universal and purchased accommodation and park tickets together.

The park which is open for Early Park Admission is usually announced in advance on the website. During busier periods, both parks may be open for EPA.

How do I get Early Park Admission?

For those staying at any on-site Universal hotel you must show your room key to gain early admission to the parks. If this is on your arrival date, then make sure you check in before Early Admission starts and then go over to the parks – when you check in you will be given a room key to show at the park entrance; your room will not be ready but you will have Early Access to one or both parks. You may be sent a text message with your room number later on - if you do not receive it, simply stop by the front desk to get your room number.

For those with a Universal Vacation Package staying off-site you do not need to check in to your hotel room, simply go straight to the Will Call kiosks located by the entrance to each park - here you can enter your confirmation number given to you when booking to redeem your tickets with Early Park Admission. We advise you bring your "E-Travel Document" which was also given to you when you booked the package. This proves that you are entitled to this benefit in case there are any problems at the turnstiles.

Entry is one hour before regular park opening – meaning early entry is allowed from 8:00am most of the year (with the parks opening for regular guests at 9:00am), and 7:00am during peak season.

Character Meet & Greets

Meeting characters can be one of the most enjoyable parts of the day in a theme park for many visitors – luckily, at Universal Orlando, there are many characters to meet. Usually the characters have little-to-no queues, unlike those at Disney, which makes the experience even better.

At *Universal's Islands of Adventure* in *Marvel Superhero Island* you will usually find Captain America, Dr. Doom, The Green Goblin, Spiderman, Storm and Wolverine. They even make their appearances (and disappearances) on cool quad bikes most of the time. You can also meet the Seuss characters at *Seuss Landing* including Cat in the Hat, the Grinch, the Lorax and even Thing 1 and 2!

At *Universal Studios Florida* you will find the characters from The Simpsons including Bart, Lisa, Homer, Marge, Krusty the Clown and Sideshow Bob all in the new Simpsons mini-land, you will also see the Blues Brothers, the Men in Black, Shrek, Fiona and Donkey, Barney, SpongeBob, the Minions and Gru, and the Transformers characters regularly around the park in areas outside their respective attractions. There are also other characters that occasionally make appearances such as Scooby Doo and Shaggy, Lucy Ball, Woody Woodpecker, Betty Boop, and Marilyn Monroe.

You can find out what times a certain character will be out by looking at your park map which will have character times listed. Some characters will not be listed on the map such as Scooby Doo but will make periodic appearances in the parks' Character Zones - these are located near the turnstiles at *Universal Studios Florida*, and in the *Toon Lagoon* area at *Islands of Adventure*.

Operating Hours and Ride Closures

The Universal Orlando Resort is open 365 days a year — as such the operating hours of the parks vary according to demand. On days when there are expected to be a lot of visitors, the parks are open longer, and when there aren't so many, the parks close earlier. The parks will always operate for their advertised operating hours. We strongly advise that you check these in advance of your visit – they may change closer to the date of your visit, so do re-check again.

Park operating hours can be verified up to two months in advance at https://www.universalorlando.com/Resort-Information/Theme-Park-Hours.aspx.

Ride refurbishments also happen throughout the year in order to keep rides operating safely and efficiently. As the Universal Orlando Resort is open 365 days a year, it does not close for several weeks or months at a time to refurbish rides like some other theme parks. Therefore, rides and attractions must close throughout the year in order to be renewed. Refurbishments tend to avoid the busier times of the year. Be sure to check in advance to avoid disappointment. Unfortunately, ride closures are only published a month or so in advance - these can be checked on the same web page as the operating hours.

Remember, as well as planned refurbishments, rides may close for technical issues or weather reasons – this is for your safety, and the engineers will do everything possible to get the ride back up as quickly as possible. There is no need to be angry at the ride attendants, as they have no control over whether the ride runs or not.

Ride Height Requirements

Many attractions at the Universal Orlando Resort have height requirements meaning that not everyone in your party may be able to enjoy every attraction. Height requirements are put in place for the safety of all guests by ensuring they fit in the ride vehicles correctly. You will need to be measured at the entrance to each ride by a ride operator if you may be close to the height limit – their word is final.

This section helpfully lists all attractions (except those without height requirements) in ascending order of height. Next to each attraction name you will find USF or IOA denoting whether the attraction is in Universal Studios Florida or in Universal's Islands of Adventure.

- **Shrek 4-D (USF)** – No minimum height restriction but no handheld infants allowed.
- **E.T. Adventure (USF)** – 34 inches (0.87m)
- **Pteranodon Flyers (IOA)** – The minimum height is 36 inches (0.92m). Guests over 56 inches (1.43m) must be accompanied by someone under 36 inches (0.92m) to ride.
- **Woody Woodpecker's Nuthouse Coaster (USF)** – 36 inches (0.92m)
- **Flight of the Hippogriff (IOA)** – 36 inches (0.92m)
- **The Cat in the Hat (IOA)** – 36 inches (0.92m) minimum to ride with an adult, or 48 inches (1.22m) to ride alone
- **The Amazing Adventures of Spider-Man (IOA)** – 40 inches (1.02m)
- **Despicable Me: Minion Mayhem (USF)** – 40 inches (1.02m)
- **TRANSFORMERS: The Ride-3D (USF)** – 40 inches (1.02m)
- **The Simpsons Ride (USF)** – 40 inches (1.02m)
- **The High in the Sky Seuss Trolley Train Ride (IOA)** – 40 inches (1.02m) minimum to ride with an adult, or 48 inches (1.22m) to ride alone
- **MEN IN BLACK: Alien Attack (USF)** – 42 inches (1.07m)
- **Popeye & Bluto's Bilge-Rat Barges (IOA)** – 42 inches (1.07m)
- **Jurassic Park River Adventure (IOA)** – 42 inches (1.07m)
- **Harry Potter and the Escape from Gringotts (USF)** – 42 inches (1.07m)
- **Dudley Do-Right Ripsaw Falls (IOA)** – 44 inches (1.12m)
- **Storm Force Accelatron** – An adult must accompany those under 48 inches (1.22m)
- **Revenge of the Mummy (USF)** – 48 inches (1.22m)
- **One Fish, Two Fish, Red Fish, Blue Fish (IOA)** – Children under 48 inches (1.22m) must ride with an adult
- **Harry Potter and the Forbidden Journey (IOA)** – 48 inches (1.22m)
- **Hollywood Rip Ride Rockit (USF)** – Minimum 51 inches (1.29m) / Maximum 79 inches (2.00m)
- **Doctor Doom's Fearfall (IOA) - 52 inches (1.32m)**
- **Dragon Challenge (IOA)** – 54 inches (1.37m)
- **The Incredible Hulk Coaster (IOA)** – 54 inches (1.37m)

Chapter 13

Comparing Universal Orlando and Walt Disney World

Universal Orlando cannot be studied in a vacuum as it is not the only theme park in Orlando. Far from it; if it were not for the other big competitor in the district, Universal most likely would not even have built a theme park in Florida. We are of course referring to the Walt Disney World Resort - the world's most visited tourist destination. There is no doubt that, one day, Universal would like to greet just as many guests as Disney does.

The two resorts – Universal Orlando and Walt Disney World – can be compared. There are many similarities and many differences, so if you have visited one and not the other, this section should be able to provide you with some sort of insight into what to expect. We hope this will help you be more prepared for your Universal Orlando experience.

Resort size – Universal Orlando resort is but a needle in a haystack in comparison to Walt Disney World. Disney covers 47 square miles, an area twice the size of Manhattan. Universal Orlando in comparison is about 1 square mile in size. Yes, it is a much smaller resort but be aware there are both advantages and disadvantages to this.

Walt Disney World hosts four theme parks, two water parks, golf and mini-golf courses, almost thirty resort hotels, dozens of miles of roads, lakes, a shopping district and much, much more. It is also important to note that Disney has only developed one third of its 47 square miles. Even so, Disney's currently developed property real estate is about 15 times larger than Universal's. Universal Orlando Resort has two theme parks, five resort hotels, and a shopping district which is significantly smaller than Disney's.

This means that Walt Disney World Resort naturally has more things to do; it has the scope to create larger developments – just Animal Kingdom Park alone at Walt Disney World is about 580 acres in size for example. The whole of Universal Orlando's land can fit in Animal Kingdom and its parking lot. This does not mean that Universal has not done a lot with the land it owns. In many ways, due to the land restriction, Universal Orlando has been far more efficient with the space it has.

The sheer size of the resort does also mean that it can take an eternity to get anywhere at Walt Disney World – you may be staying at an on-site hotel but it can easily be a 20-minute bus journey to the theme parks. Whereas, at Universal you are much closer to the action and can catch a boat to the theme parks from most hotels in a matter or minutes, or simply walk everywhere.

Lastly, it is important to note that because of its size you are much more likely to spend one, two or even three weeks at Walt Disney World Resort, whereas you would struggle to fill more than four or five days at Universal Orlando.

Planning – A vacation/holiday to Walt Disney World cannot be done without A LOT of planning – you need to research which ticket type you want, which of the resort hotels you want to stay at (there are over 25 to choose from), which theme park you want to visit on which day, and potentially have to book your restaurants 180 days before you even step foot on Disney property. You then best have a strategy about which rides to do when, know the ins and outs of the Fastpass+ system and know what times the characters meet and greet to make the most of your time – you will even need to make ride and show reservations 30 to 60 days in advance to get the most out of your ticket.

A Universal Orlando Resort vacation *does* require some planning; we won't lie to you. We are sure you know that because you have purchased this guide. It does, however, not require anywhere near the degree of planning that a Walt Disney World vacation does. You can take it more at your own pace. There are only five on-site hotels to choose from which greatly reduces the time looking at those, though there are many nearby off-site hotels you could consider. Ticket options are simpler: you simply decide how many days and whether you want to park-hop or not. Restaurants can be booked much closer to the day or even on the day itself, but definitely not 180 days out like at Disney.

As far as having a strategy of what rides and experiences you do when, we recommend that you have one for all theme parks – Universal Orlando included. However, you will not need to make ride reservations for Universal Orlando like you do at Disney, because this is simply not possible. Follow our touring plans, or if you have Express Pass access simply enjoy the attractions in whatever order you want.

There is still *some* planning to do for a Universal Orlando Resort vacation but it is a lot less than at Walt Disney World.

Off-Season – We all know that visiting the theme parks during school breaks means that they are going to be busy; the kids are out of school and parents want them to have fun so the theme parks are naturally going to be filled with guests. What about out of season? Like September during school time, or February. At Walt Disney World you can expect to find crowds year round – there are quieter days than others, but there is never going to be a day at Walt Disney World you can walk into the Magic Kingdom and stroll onto Seven Dwarfs Mine Train within 5 minutes; it is simply never going to happen – especially at Magic Kingdom Park.

This is different at Universal Orlando; there are still lots of times of the year in off-season when almost every ride is a walk-on – these are times when you can experience *Harry Potter and the Forbidden Journey* in a matter or minutes instead of hours! The off-season still exists at Universal. We think this may have a lot to do with the target demographic of Universal with older teens likely being in school for longer, whereas very young kids are often not in school and can visit Disney year-round. At the same time Walt Disney World also generally appeals more to the local, older, retired population than Universal Orlando, so it attracts them year-round too.

Having said this, if Universal Orlando continues to soar in popularity as it has done in recent years, it is very possible that the same situation will develop at Universal Orlando, particularly as the parks have a very limited number of attractions. In 2014, for example, the Universal Orlando Resort theme parks welcomed 7.9% - or 1.2 million - more guests than they did the year prior. In 2013, there was an increase of 1 million guests across the resort. The parks are getting busier at Universal Orlando, just nowhere near as busy as at Disney.

Character meet and greets – At the Walt Disney World Resort, you have to plan which characters you want to meet and when, even with the possibility of making FastPass+ reservations. At Universal Orlando, its more spontaneous and you should never have to wait more than a 5 or 10-minutes to meet a character. Compare that to a 180-minute wait for the princesses in Disney's *Magic Kingdom* and you can see the difference.

Hotel accommodation – We touched on this briefly earlier on in the 'resort size' section. Hotels on-site at Universal Orlando are physically much closer to the parks than those at Walt Disney World. However, there are fewer choices and the three top hotels are expensive, though Cabana Bay and Sapphire Falls offer a more reasonable value and moderate price range. The flip side is that there are off-site hotels located a 2-minute drive away or a 15-minute walk, for a wider variety of option. This is not the case at Walt Disney World where offsite hotels are a considerable distance away.

You're not locked in at Universal – This is related to our previous point. You can actually walk off-site at Universal Orlando and leave the area. You can walk to a Walgreens if you want. If you make the effort, you can go and eat outside of the Universal Orlando Resort and make significant savings on the price of food, as well as the price of accommodation. This is simply not possible at Walt Disney World without a car, and a lot more time and hassle.

Innovative attractions at Universal – This one will be controversial from the view of many Disney aficionados but in our opinion Universal is developing many more innovative and revolutionary experiences that Disney is simply missing out on. Yes, Walt Disney World has some incredible revolutionary experiences of its own - *Test Track, Soarin', Mickey's Philharmagic, Kilimanjaro Safaris, Rock n Rollercoaster,* and the *Tower of Terror* to name but a few.

The last big revolution for Disney, in our opinion, was *Expedition Everest* in 2006 – ten years ago. If we wanted to be generous, we would add *Seven Dwarfs Mine Train* and *Enchanted Tales with Belle* too which opened in 2014 and 2012 respectively.

However, in the same timespan, Universal Orlando has blown Disney out of the water. Universal Orlando only opened in 1990 and the resort is dotted with innovative experiences - *The Incredible Hulk Coaster* wins coaster awards year after year, the same can be said for *The Amazing Adventures of Spider-Man.* There is *Rip Ride Rockit, Harry Potter and the Forbidden Journey, Harry Potter and the Escape from Gringotts, Hogwarts Express, The Simpsons Ride, Dueling Dragons, Jurassic Park River Adventure* and many more incredible experiences.

The attractions that have opened at Universal Orlando over the past few years are immense, and there are new attractions and experiences opening every year for the foreseeable future.

This may all change in 2016 with the opening of the new Frozen attraction in EPCOT and in 2017 with Avatar Land, but Universal will be counteracting with a King Kong attraction in 2016, and a slew of new attractions in 2017.

Lockers – Just a small quirk, but it is something to get used to and be aware of. Whereas at Walt Disney World you can take your belongings onto every single ride and keep them at your feet or in your pockets, at Universal Orlando Resort you must leave them in (free) lockers whilst you are riding select attractions. This can be an annoying process, though admittedly it is safer for guests.

Friendliness – Although Universal Orlando has recently improved on the friendliness of Team Members; their employees are still nothing like Disney's. Disney's Cast Members are empowered to "make magical moments" to improve anyone's vacation the way Universal employees just are not. Disney employees seem happier, and have "courtesy" employed as one of 4 key values that must always be followed.

At Disney's parks the only reason the courtesy of an employee to be compromised would be in a safety-critical situation, otherwise the Cast Members cannot do enough for you - most will go above and beyond, and provide exceptional customer service.

Universal Orlando on the other hand provides good service for the most part and most of the Team Members are great but it seems that all too often during a visit these employees are overshadowed by those who are nonchalant at best, and rude at worst. Your mileage may vary, but Disney has the edge here.

Live entertainment – You would think for a company that is celebrating 100 years of movies Universal would know how to put on a good show or two. They do - just not at the Universal Orlando Resort. The *Universal Studios Hollywood* park in California is filled with great shows yet sadly none have made their way across to Orlando. A rare exception is the live entertainment in the *Diagon Alley* section of the park, which is outstanding. Shows like *SindBad* and *Fear Factor* are old, not relevant to the younger generation, and are aging badly. In comparison, shows like *Dream Along with Mickey, Finding Nemo the Musical* and *The Festival of the Lion King* are masterpieces.

Unfortunately, it is the same story with parades and fireworks – although better than many other theme parks, Universal Orlando Resort's offerings are nowhere near as good as any of Disney's parades or nighttime shows.

FASTPASS+ vs. Express Pass – At Walt Disney World Resort your park ticket enables you access to make free Fastpass+ reservations, which let you skip the regular queue lines by giving you a certain time to ride. You can make these in advance or on the day of your visit itself – if made in advance it is a good way of guaranteeing that you will experience some of your favorite attractions. It is a bit of a complicated system to understand but guidebooks like *The Independent Guide to Walt Disney World 2016* go through the whole process in detail.

Express Pass at Universal Orlando allows you near-instant entry to almost all attractions for a fee – this fee can be very high and up to $135 per person per day, or free if you are staying at certain on-site hotels.

Leaving aside the fact that Disney's FastPass+ is obviously much better value as it is free, Universal's Express Pass because of its paid nature works better: there is rarely more than a 10-minute wait, you do not make reservations in advance, there is no complicated system to understand, less people use it and it is available for almost every single attraction. It really is an 'express pass' at Universal Orlando because there's no need to go back and forth between attractions and make reservations, you simply turn up and skip the main queue.

Target Audience – This is one of the most striking differences between the two resorts. Universal Orlando Resort caters more towards teenagers and adults; Walt Disney World Resort doing have thrill rides but mainly targets families and younger kids.

With the exception of rides like *Rock 'N' Rollercoaster, Tower of Terror, Expedition Everest, Mission: SPACE* and *Test Track*, there are few things that will get the adrenaline rushing for teenagers at the Walt Disney World Resort. Disney caters more towards the families with experiences such as *Soarin', Big Thunder Mountain, Kilimanjaro Safaris* and character experiences uniting the whole family. At the same time the really small ones can enjoy classics such as *Peter Pan's Flight* and *it's a small world*.

Universal Orlando Resort is very different. There are a few things for the younger members of the family, but for the most part it is high intensity thrills that people come to Universal Orlando for, as well as big family adventures. *The Incredible Hulk Coaster, Dueling Dragons, Hollywood Rip Ride Rockit* and *Dr. Doom's Fear Fall* are just a few of the thrilling experiences on offer.

The family rides at Universal Orlando are generally more adult-oriented too: *Harry Potter and the Forbidden Journey* and *Harry Potter and the Escape from Gringotts* are most thrilling than most rides at Disney, and the same can be said for *The Amazing Adventures of Spider-Man*, *The Simpsons* and *Transformers: The Ride*. Although there are some attractions for the smaller members of the family such as *Barney*, and numerous playground areas, these are few and far between at Universal Orlando Resort.

Less strollers – This is another minor consideration, but the fact that there are more adults and teenagers at Universal Orlando Resort means that one advantage is that you do not have to swim through a sea of strollers or pushchairs to get to your favorite attraction. Strollers and small children are well accepted throughout the parks but there are simply fewer of them.

Dining – Food at Universal Orlando is generally slightly cheaper than at Walt Disney World. There is nowhere near as much variety at Universal Orlando as there is at Walt Disney World though; you will pretty much have to stick to standard theme park food. The biggest difference in our opinion, however, is the quality and taste; whilst food at the Disney's parks is not gourmet by any standard in general it is much better than Universal Orlando's.

There are also a lot fewer table service establishments at Universal Orlando, so if you fancy a sit-down meal your options are much more limited here. At Disney character buffets and table service meals are part of the experience (and whilst people are eating, they aren't in the increasing wait times in the queue lines).

Water Rides – If you have ridden *Splash Mountain* at the *Magic Kingdom* in Disney World and you came out a little bit wet, this is nothing compared to the water attractions at Universal Orlando! Go on a water ride at Universal's parks and you will not be coming out having been sprayed or splashed, you will come out drenched. Universal Orlando really does like to soak you on these rides, and Universal's *Islands of Adventure* is the perfect place to do this with three major water attractions.

Resort transportation – We touched on this briefly before, but due to the size of Walt Disney World, there are various ways of getting to and from the theme parks to your hotel, all depending on where their locations. There are ferryboats, buses and monorails varying how you can get to the parks – some of these trips lake you forgot you are at a theme park resort due to how calming and serene they can be.

However, journey times at Walt Disney World Resort can vary from just a few minutes to 25 minutes or more. You may also require several transfers for certain trips. You can also walk between some limited areas of the Walt Disney World Resort but for the most part you will need to take their free resort transportation, or drive.

Universal Orlando Resort also allows everyone to use its resort transportation for free. This is made up of a fleet of water taxis, which take you to and from the *CityWalk* area and three of the on-site hotels. The boat journeys should not take more than 10 minutes.

Otherwise, you can use the walking paths to walk across the entire Universal Orlando Resort (this is impossible to do at Disney, with many areas not allowing pedestrian traffic), or use the scheduled bus transportation.

Nightlife – As far as nightlife is concerned, Universal Orlando hands-down beats Walt Disney World. Universal Orlando has a much wider variety of clubs and bars, and is truly considered a party scene. Walt Disney World does not do badly with some bars and a club in the *Disney Springs* area, but it is just nowhere near the scale of Universal Orlando's offerings. Both resorts host a large-scale nighttime paid admission show – Blue Man at Universal Orlando, and Cirque du Soleil at Walt Disney World.

Special events – Both Universal and Disney know that in order to keep people coming to the Resorts all year-round, they need to offer different events year-round.

As far as Halloween is concerned, Universal Orlando offers a much scarier portrayal of the season with *Halloween Horror Nights*, Disney goes for a "not so scary" approach.

Christmas, however, is a much bigger deal at Walt Disney World than at Universal Orlando with all four of the theme parks celebrating it through unique shows, decorations, lighting ceremonies and even stories from around the world at EPCOT. Even the resort hotels get in to the spirit, with Christmas trees and gingerbread houses.

Universal Orlando holds its own unique events throughout the year such as Mardi Gras and the concert series. Disney holds concerts too and celebrates the Flower and Garden festival, and the Food and Wine festival. Both resorts celebrate the countdown to the New Year in style.

Chapter 14

Seasonal Events:

The Universal Orlando Resort offers something different all year round. Whether it is live entertainment, horror mazes or Holiday cheer, the Universal team have it all covered. This section covers all of the seasonal events that happen throughout the year.

25th Anniversary Concert Series

November 2015

May/June 2016 (to be confirmed)

The *25th Anniversary Concert series* is an opportunity to check out some big acts in the park whilst getting some ride time in too. The *Universal Music Plaza* stage area near *Rip Ride Rockit* has bands playing on select dates. There is no extra charge to listen to the live music and there can be some pretty big bands - all you need is your regular park admission ticket to get in. There is no seating area for the concert; it is all standing room.

Concerts take place on Saturdays and Sundays and several big acts have ben announced: Jason Deluro (7:00pm – Nov 14th), Colbie Callait (7:00pm – Nov 21st), Flo Rida (8pm – Nov 22nd), Carly Rae Jepsen (8pm – Nov 27th) and Daughtry (8pm – Nov 28th).

It is unclear if you will be able to purchase Concert Only admission to the theme park.

In the past when this was offered, a concert ticket could be purchased for $69.99 - this allowed you into the park from 7:00pm until park closing. Once inside you can either watch the concert or experience the attractions or a combination of both. Do note that arriving at 7:00pm would *not* get you front row standing room for the concerts.

The concert series usually takes place in the summer and we expect this event to return in May and June 2016.

The Christmas and the Holiday Season

December

There is a surprising amount on offer during the Holiday season at the Universal Orlando Resort. Unlike the season at Walt Disney World which runs from November, the Holiday season at Universal Orlando is shorter. In 2015 it runs from December 5th 2015 to January 2nd 206. The dates are always similar every year, give or take a few days.

Thanksgiving

Although the theme parks do not have any special events for Thanksgiving, the on-site hotels do offer Thanksgiving celebrations:

- Cabana Bay Beach Resort will host a special dinner on Thanksgiving and the Macy's Thanksgiving Day Parade will be shown on the big screens at Bayline diner.

- Loews Royal Pacific Resort will host a Holiday buffet on Thanksgiving Day with Universal Orlando characters present and other live entertainment. This is priced at $56 per adult and $24 per child. A special Wantilan Luau will take place on the 28th November 2015 which includes all the regular Polynesian food and entertainment, plus a special tree lighting ceremony.

- The Hard Rock Hotel Orlando will also host a Holiday buffet on Thanksgiving Day with Universal Orlando characters present and other live entertainment. This is priced at $58 per adult and $20 for children.

- Loews Portofino Bay Hotel will offer a buffet in the Tuscan Ballroom with live entertainment, priced at $70 per adult and $26.50 per child. Trattoria del Porto will also offer a holiday buffet with live entertainment (plus Universal Orlando characters) for $63 per adult and $18 per child. Finally, on 27th November 2015 Holiday Harbor Nights is a special event with wine, gourmet food and jazz entertainment, as well as an illumination of the resort's main Christmas tree. Tickets start at $45, with VIP tickets priced at $75.

Christmas

At *Universal Studios Florida* watch as the Macy's Holiday Parade rolls through the streets with floats taken from the world-famous full-scale Thanksgiving Day Parade in New York City. This event runs every evening throughout the holiday season. For the best position, get a spot in the New York area of the park facing the Christmas tree. This is because when Santa comes past, he'll light up the tree as a special bonus surprise.

Top Tip: You can sign up as a balloon handler and help carry the balloons around the parade route for an extra special souvenir. There are several restrictions as far as being in good health, wearing closed toe shoes, being over 48 inches tall, and you must be over 18 to participate. Sign up takes place two hours before the parade begins in the Woody Woodpecker's KidZone area of the park where there is a big teddy bear waiting for you.

You will also find live band "Mannheim steamroller" – the biggest selling Christmas band of all time – rocking the stage with live performances on December 5th, 6th, 12th, 13th, 19th and 20th in 2015 – each performance will begin at 6:00pm and run for approximately one hour. In addition, Barney's *"A Day in the Park with Barney"* show gets a Christmas twist and runs multiple times each day, as does *The Blue's Brothers (Holiday) Show.*

At *Islands of Adventure* the Holiday fun continues. Watch the fantastic *"Grinchmas Who-liday Spectacular"* – a 30-minute live-show with great music and starring The Grinch himself, telling you the story of how he stole Christmas. If you fancy something to eat, then why not meet the Dr Seuss characters at the holiday-season-only Character Breakfast with Grinch and Friends - reservations are required for this one. Finally, you can actually meet The Grinch himself. Play, laugh and get some great photos!

Unfortunately, there are no meet and greets with Santa Claus at either park throughout the Holiday season. This is a bit of a missed opportunity if you ask us.

However, the celebration continues at the on-site hotels. At the resorts, you check out holiday buffets and dining events, tree-lighting ceremonies, special music performances, Hanukkah candle lightings, visits from Santa Claus, holiday poolside "dive-in" movies and family-friendly New Year's Eve celebrations.

New Year's Eve
For the transition into the New Year head over to *CityWalk* and party the night away with live performances and a midnight champagne toast! The New Year's Even entertainment is not complimentary and you must purchase a ticket to access the area for this evening.

The New Year's Eve party includes admission to six clubs, six party zones, a pyrotechnics display, unlimited gourmet cuisine, a midnight champagne toast and much more. It is one of the year's biggest events and tickets run from $105 to $135 per person plus tax. This party is for over 21s only. A VIP package is also available for $145 to $185 per person, plus tax – this includes private VIP areas throughout CityWalk (excludes Cabanas), exclusive food stations, drink specials, private bars and seating areas.

Alternatively, Hard Rock Live Orlando will be hosting their own New Year Eve's party from 8:00pm priced at $85 to $95 per person, and $145 for the VIP package.

The theme parks themselves do not have any special entertainment for New Year's Eve – they will be open late, though, with Islands of Adventure closing at 11:00pm and Universal Studios Florida closing at 1:00am. Universal's Cinematic Spectacular nighttime show will be performed at 11:59pm on New Year's Eve.

The on-site hotels will also host their own parties:
- Cabana Bay Beach Resort will host an event at Bayline Diner which is complimentary and will include a balloon drop at midnight, food and drinks, face painting and a DJ. Entry is free but food, drinks, and face painting are paid activities.
- Loews Royal Pacific Resort will hold a New Year's Eve Champagne & Cocktail Reception. This will include h'ors d'ouevres, a live DJ, a live stream of the ball drop, and a champagne toast at midnight. Entry is $38 for adult and $22 per child, plus tax. At the New Year's Eve Wantilan Luau you can celebrate New Year with a buffet, alcoholic and non alcoholic drinks, a tree lighting, fire dancers, hula dancers and live music. Pricing is $85 per adult and $35 per child.
- The Hard Rock Hotel hosts the "Rock-in 2016 Holiday Buffet & Lobby Party" where you can enjoy multiple food and dessert stations, a live stream of Times Square, a DJ spinning holiday songs, Universal Orlando characters, a midnight toast and more. Pricing is $99 for adults and $45 for children. If you only want the lobby party, without the buffet, pricing is $60 per adult and $35 per child.
- Loews Portofino Bay Hotel will hold a New Year's Party in the Piazza with multiple food stations, a kids' buffet, complimentary wines, a DJ spinning holiday tunes, a midnight toast and more. Pricing is $145 per adult and $35 per child.

At the time of writing, the 2016 Holiday season is over a year away, and it is difficult to predict exactly what will be taking place at the time. However, Universal Orlando Resort has been very consistent with its Holiday season over the years, and we would expect all the above events to take place again in 2016.

A Celebration of Harry Potter

January 29th to 31st 2016

The 'Celebration of Harry Potter' event first ran at Universal Orlando in 2014 and has returned every year since. This year you can once again expect three full days of Wizarding fun. During the event you can see talent from the Harry Potter film who will take part in live Q&As, watch panels and demonstrations, and explore the large Expo area.

Most of the events which are part of this three-day celebration are included in regular park admission and carry no additional charge. These are three magical days no Harry Potter fan will want to miss.

Film stars and autographs:

Several Harry Potter film stars will be present throughout the event. For 2016 you will be able to see: Rupert Grint (Ron Weasley), Bonnie Wright (Ginny Weasley), Katie Leung (Cho Chang), Matthew Lewis (Neville Longbottom) and Evanna Lynch (Luna Lovegood).

A Celebration of Harry Potter Expo:

Make your way through interactive displays in this unique collection of Harry Potter themed props, movie sets, artwork and more. This year, Universal Orlando will welcome *back Harry Potter: The Exhibition, Warner Bros. Studio Tour London, MinaLima, Pottermore.com, Scholastic,* and *Warner Bros.* as part of the A Celebration of Harry Potter Expo. These are the events which will be part of the Expo in 2016:

- **Harry Potter: The Exhibition** – At the beginning of each school year the Sorting Hat sorts new Hogwarts students into their houses, and you'll have the opportunity to get sorted in a Hogwarts-inspired setting. Step inside the Expo and the red carpet is rolled out welcoming you to an area celebrating to the global impact *Harry Potter: The Exhibition* has had during its 7-year, 12-city tour, including an exclusive Quidditch inspired photo opportunity.

- **Warner Bros. Studio Tour London: The Making of Harry Potter** – Based at the production home of the Harry Potter film series, Warner Bros. Studio Tour London gives you the chance to step onto the actual sets used during filming, as well as costumes and props. The Studio Tour is bringing an interactive mini-tour experience to the event, giving you the chance to see the incredible behind-the-scenes talent that went into creating the iconic films.

- **MinaLima** – Graphic designers Miraphora Mina and Eduardo Lima worked for ten years on the Harry Potter films, creating countless pieces of unforgettable artwork, some of which will be on display, including the Marauder's Map, Daily Prophet, and Hogwarts school books.

- **Pottermore from J.K. Rowling** – Pottermore is the digital heart of J.K. Rowling's Wizarding World and if discovering more about her magical universe excites you, Pottermore has a surprise in store for fans attending this year's event. Keep your eyes peeled for their new Pottermore Correspondent (Rita Skeeter she certainly isn't), who'll be there hunting out exclusive scoops and bringing you updates on pottermore.com from the weekend's activities.

- **Scholastic** – Meet award-winning illustrator Kazu Kibuishi, who reimagined the Harry Potter book covers.

- **Warner Bros.** – Celebrate Harry Potter at Scholastic's booth by sharing a message about what Harry Potter means to you. Color in a magical page from our brand-new Harry Potter coloring book. Be sure to enter daily raffles for a chance to win a copy of the new illustrated edition of *Harry Potter and the Sorcerer's Stone*, a box set of all seven Harry Potter books, or a Harry Potter coloring book. Collectible giveaways available for Potter fans of all ages.

Discussions & Demonstrations

As well as the Expo, guests can enjoy several panels and demonstrations. Here are the ones which have been confirmed for 2016:

- **Behind the Scenes: Harry Potter Film Talent Q&A** – Enjoy a fascinating and interactive question and answer session featuring some of your favorite actors from the Harry Potter films. Discover what it was like to work on one of the most successful film franchises in history.

- **The Global Impact of Harry Potter: The Exhibition** – Celebrate the touring attraction that has visited 13 cities in 9 countries and hosted almost 4 million guests. *Harry Potter: The Exhibition* is in a unique position to reflect on the global impact of the franchise. Get an exclusive look at the exhibition's creation and the excitement it continues to deliver to fans around the world. Panel will include exhibition creators, film producers, and film actors who have participated in the openings.

- **Graphic Design for the Harry Potter Films with MinaLima** – Miraphora Mina and Eduardo Lima, from the graphic design studio MinaLima, will share insights into their role as graphic prop designers, and how their paths crossed at the WB film studios to work for 10 years on the Harry Potter movies. They will discuss and show some of the iconic props they created for the Harry Potter films, including The Marauder's Map, the Daily Prophet, and The

Quibbler, amongst others. Still immersed in all things Harry Potter, they will also talk about their recent involvement in the Wizarding World of Harry Potter - Diagon Alley, for which they designed all the street and store graphics. During the panel they will welcome questions from the audience.

- **Harry Potter Props Showcase with Acclaimed Prop Maker Pierre Bohanna** – Ever wondered how long it takes to make a wand? Or the inspiration for the hundreds of wand designs in the Harry Potter film series? Warner Bros. *Studio Tour London – The Making of Harry Potter* presents head prop maker, Pierre Bohanna, who will answer these questions and many more. Remember to bring along your wand as there may be a masked visitor or two during the showcase.

Demonstrations For The Younger Fans (Recommended for Ages 12 and Under)
- **Dance Like a Beauxbatons & Battle Like a Durmstrang** – If your younger Harry Potter fans are entranced by the dances performed by Beauxbatons and Durmstrang students in the Harry Potter films, they will love this demonstration. A Universal Orlando choreographer will explain the movements and techniques behind the mesmerizing dance routines.
- **Harry Potter Film Trivia** – How well do your children (or you) know the Harry Potter films? Test your knowledge during this fun audience-interaction game inviting younger fans to shout out the answers to film-specific questions. Perhaps a Harry Potter film marathon is in order before trying your luck?

Mardi Gras
Select nights in Spring. Exact 2016 dates not yet announced.
Celebrate New Orleans with Universal Orlando's Mardi Gras celebrations. The event traditionally runs on select nights from February to April each year. The exact dates for 2016 were not available at the time of writing. Entry to Mardi Gras is included in your regular park admission.

Live concerts are the name of the game with the *Music Plaza stage* hosting live acts on select nights. The line up for 2015 included: Olivia Newton-John, Jessie J, Barenaked Ladies, Kelly Clarkson, Heart, Trace Adkins, The All-American Rejects, Trey Songz, and many others.

As well as the bands on the main stage, there will also be New Orleans Bands performing the French Quarter Courtyard. There are also stalls with local cuisine including jambalaya and gumbo. This area opens at 4:00pm and closes at the concert start time.

There is no seating area for the concerts: it is all general standing room. For the best view of the Music Plaza Stage concerts you will need to skip the Mardi Gras Parade (more on this later) altogether or watch it from as close to the Music Plaza stage area as possible.

The highlight of the festivities for many is the Mardi Gras Parade with colorful floats and incredible music - be prepared for the traditional throwing of the beads from the floats for you to catch.

After the parks are shut, head to the CityWalk bars and clubs for more New Orleans-inspired fun.

Top Tip: Note that when the parade starts, the regular shows and attractions at the park will stop operating for the day.

Important Note: The Universal Cinematic Spectacular did not take place on Mardi Gras nights in 2014 or 2015. We do not expect it to take place in 2016 either.

Grad Bash
8th, 15th, 23rd and 29th April 2016
Universal's *Grad Bash* is when High School Seniors get to celebrate their graduation in style at both Universal Orlando theme parks.

The event runs from 7:00pm to 2:00am. Tickets allow entry into both theme parks and also allow entry into one of two pre-parties: *CityWalk* (5:00pm-8:00pm), or *Universal Studios Florida* (5:00pm-7:00pm). Both pre-parties include a buffet dinner and entertainment.

During the *Grad Bash* night itself there are live concerts (including Jessie J and Jason Derulo in 2016), karaoke sessions, dance parties, street entertainment and the chance to experience some thrilling attractions. A dress code is enforced during the event.

Some of the attractions operating during Grad Bash include both sides of the Wizarding World of Harry Potter, TRANSFORMERS: The Ride–3D, Despicable Me Minion Mayhem, The Amazing Adventures of Spider-Man, The Incredible Hulk Coaster and more attractions. That means that Grad Night guests get access to both theme parks!

More information can be obtained be emailing GradBash@UniversalOrlando.com or over the phone on 1-800-YOUTH15. Although ticket prices vary from school to school expect to pay around the $120 mark.

Gradventure

6th, 13th and 20th May 2015

Gradventure is the opportunity for middle school kids to celebrate their graduation in style. With both theme parks open for the event, it is an experience unlikely any other in the world. Visitors can ride world-class rides and enjoy private theme park admission.

The event runs from 7:00pm to midnight. At the *Gradventure* night itself there are Live DJs in attendance, Karaoke sessions, dance parties, street entertainment and of course the chance to experience some thrilling attractions.

Some of the attractions operating during Gradventure include both sides of the Wizarding World of Harry Potter and the Hogwarts Express, TRANSFORMERS: The Ride–3D, Despicable Me Minion Mayhem, The Amazing Adventures of Spider-Man, The Incredible Hulk Coaster and more attractions. That means that Grad Night guests get access to both theme parks!

More information can be obtained be emailing Gradventure@UniversalOrlando.com or over the phone on 1-800-YOUTH15. Although ticket prices vary from school to school expect to pay around the $75 mark.

Rock the Universe

September 2016

Billed as "Florida's Biggest Christian Music Festival", *Rock the Universe* is a weekend where you can learn about Christian faith and worship, all with Christian rock music of course. Select attractions also operate during the event.

There is also a free Sunday Morning Worship Service led by a guest speaker for those who hold *Rock the Universe* tickets. Reservations are required. Dates for 2016 have not yet been announced and the line-up is usually released in April each year.

As well as the main stage which will feature Christian acts, the Coca-Cola FanZone features more live music, as well as band autograph sessions, karaoke, and more. On Saturday night, guests can enjoy the Candelighting Ceremony, followed by a morning worship service the next day.

Select attractions will also operate during the Rock the Universe event. In the past these attractions have included TRANSFORMERS: The Ride-3D, Hollywood Rip Ride Rockit, Revenge of the Mummy, and MEN IN BLACK Alien Attack. Diagon Alley was closed throughout the 2014 and 2015 events. We do not expect it to open in 2016.

Rock the Universe is a separate ticketed event and guests must pay to access the event, even if they have a ticket for that day as it operates outside of regular park hours. 2015 tickets were priced at $61.99 for one night of the event, or $99.99 for both nights of the event. For $124.99 guests could enjoy both nights of the event plus admission to the park for three full days doing one park per day. Tickets allow access to *Universal Studios Florida* between 4:00pm and 1:00am.

Finally, for $161.99 guests could enjoy both nights of the event plus admission to the park for three full days with park-to-park access for the whole weekend. These tickets offer fantastic value for money.

Top Tip: A one-night event-only Express Pass has previously been available for $16 for one use per participating attraction, or $25 for unlimited uses at participating attractions. These are a real bargain in our opinion! Either way, you can guarantee almost immediate access to your favorite rides for a small cost. We shall see if this returns in 2016.

Halloween Horror Nights
Select nights from September 16th to October 31st 2016

This is the biggest event of the year for Universal Orlando and takes place across both coasts - Hollywood and Orlando. It has been running for over 25 years.

Halloween Horror Nights is an evening extravaganza where there are heaving themed hemed haunted houses, live entertainment is on offer and there are scare zones where "scarectors" roam around to frighten you - these can be anything from zombies to madmen with chainsaws. The theming is absolutely incredible during these events and unlike any other scare attraction in the US. As well as this, you will find most of the attractions open inside Universal Studios Florida.

The only details we have for the 2016 event at this stage are the dates, but even these are subject to change: select nights from September 16th to October 31st 2016. Apart from that we have no other details as to the haunted houses on offer in 2016. More information on the 2016 event should be released between July and the end of August 2016.

Halloween Horror Nights (HHN) is very, very popular and *Universal Studios Florida* does get extremely crowded during these events. Expect to easily 90 minutes or more in line for each haunted house. This is one time when we highly recommend purchasing the *HHN* Express Pass if you want the full experience and to see everything, though it is an additional supplement of over $100 extra. Even with the Express Passes waits can regularly reach an hour, however. Alternatively, make multiple visits to see everything on offer.

Dates:
Halloween Horror Nights runs on select nights. Exact dates for 2015 have not yet been announced but Universal Orlando has revealed that the event will run from September 16th to October 31st 2016.

What is part of HHN?
Each year, the entertainment changes at Halloween Horror Nights, and that is one of the things that keeps people coming back again and again. For reference, in 2015 there were nine different haunted houses – Freddy vs Jason; Insidious; The Purge; The Walking Dead: The Living and the Dead; An American Werewolf in London; Jack Presents: 25 Years of Monsters and Mayhem; RUN: Blood, Sweat, and Fears; Asylum in Wonderland 3D; and Body Collector – Recollections.

Guests can expect the haunted houses to last about 3 to 5 minutes each. Haunted houses for 2016 have not yet been announced.

There were also five scare zones in 2015 where characters roam the zones causing fear - here you do not need to queue to be scared. In 2015 there were Psychoscareapy: Unleashed, ICONS: HHN, Scary Tales: ScreamPunk, Evil's Roots All Nite Die-In: Double Feature. Also, scattered around the park will be scare-actors with chainsaws...ready to run at you.

As far as live stage shows, 2015 saw the return of Bill & Ted's Excellent Halloween Adventure (a really enjoyable stage show) and The Carnage Returns (a show hosted by Universal's Jack the Clown character).

The following attractions were also open during HHN in 2014: TRANSFORMERS The Ride 3D, Hollywood Rip Ride Rockit, MEN IN BLACK Alien Attack, Revenge of the Mummy, The Simpsons Ride and Escape from Gringotts. Queues for attractions are generally non-existent throughout the event, as the focus is on the scare aspect of the night for many people. Guests with a HHN Express Pass can use it for both the scare zones and all the aforementioned attractions.

Universal warns the event "may be too intense for young children and is not recommended for children under the age of 13". Children under this age may come as no proof of age is requested but it is not recommended. No costumes or masks are allowed at the event.

Is The Wizarding World of Harry Potter part of HHN?
Information for the 2016 edition has not been released in regards to this – however, this is how it worked in 2015, we expect it to be similar in 2016:

Halloween Horror Nights entertainment will not extend to the Wizarding World of Harry Potter: Diagon Alley area of the park. This means that there will not be any additional 'horror' in Diagon Alley – no scare-actors, no shows, no haunted houses. However, the area will be open in its normal state meaning that *Escape from Gringotts*, the shops and the eateries will be open. This will be a safe refuge from the horror outside for anyone that needs a break.

Pricing:

Ticket sales for 2016 are not yet open. For reference, in 2015 a single **general admission ticket** was priced at $101.99 on the gate or at **http://www.halloweenhorrornights.com/orlando/tickets.html** in advance. Think this is expensive? We agree, see the other ticket options below.

HHN as an add on:

You can also add a night of Halloween Horror Nights to your daytime park ticket and save a substantial amount of money (versus purchasing them separately). Your Halloween Horror Nights ticket does not have to be used the same day as your daytime park ticket. The price in 2015 varied between $49.99 and $76.99 depending on which date your visited on. You can buy this in advance with a day ticket, or at the resort itself with a day ticket present with you at the time of purchase.

Rush of Fear Passes:

For online purchases made in advance, the **Rush of Fear** pass was priced at $83.99 and allowed entry at every event night during the first 3 weeks of 2015 for one low price. A **Rush of Fear + HHN Express Pass** option was also available which allowed you entry during the first 3 weeks of 2015 as well as allowing you to bypass the regular lines once at each of the haunted houses per night – this was priced at $229.99.

Other advanced purchase options in 2015 included the Frequent Fear, and Frequent Fear + HHN Express Pass options: these were priced between $94.99 and $297.99, depending on the dates of visit and whether they include Express Pass access or not.

HHN Express passes:

If you wish to buy separate HHN Express Passes, in 2015 these varied in price from $69.99 to $119.99 per person and are valid during the event night only for haunted houses and attractions. We recommend you buy these in advance as they will sell out for peak nights. On peak nights you *need* a HHN Express Pass to see everything, as wait times for haunted houses will typically be between 90 minutes and three hours making Express Passes a necessity, not a luxury. Note that even with an Express Pass you may have to wait an hour or more to enter the haunted houses during peak nights – it will not be instant or quick entry. Note that Express Passes purchased for daytime at Universal Orlando are not valid during HHN, nor are the Hotel Express Passes – if you want to skip the lines during HHN you will have to cough up some cash.

RIP Tours (all details for 2014):

You can get a **private VIP tour** (dubbed an 'RIP' tour during HHN) with immediate unlimited access to every haunted house and attraction (plus many other benefits) starting at $1399 for a party of 10, plus tax and the cost of HHN park admission. There are several benefits to this package and if you can get 10 people to do it, $140 each works out at outstanding value for what you get – of course that is the starting price.

If you cannot gather a group, a **public RIP tour** which includes one-time immediate access to every haunted house, plus the attractions (plus many other benefits), starting at $139.99 per person, plus the cost of HHN park admission.

For both experiences you can call for date-specific prices at 1-866-346-9350 or you can email **vipexperience@universalorlando.com**.

Guided Tours (all details for 2015):

If you want to see how the horror of HHN is created without the scares, then Universal Orlando offers a guided tour for you:

- **Unmasking the Horror Tour** – This tour will take you on a lights-on tour through three haunted houses with a guide. You will learn about the process that goes into creating these houses without the scares. Photos are permitted. The tour lasts up to 2 hour 30 minutes for groups of up to 15 guests. Tours are priced at $64.99 per person (plus tax) and there are both morning and afternoon tours. Both tours go through different haunted houses – guests who wish to see all six houses on the same day can purchase both tours at a discounted price of $109.99 per person, plus tax. These tours take place during the regular daytime hours of the park.

You can call to book at 1-866-346-9350 or email **vipexperience@universalorlando.com**.

How to get in to Halloween Horror Night 45 minutes before everyone else:

Make sure you already have a day ticket or annual pass and are in the park before 4:15pm. The park usually closes at 5:00pm for regular guests on *HHN* and guests are not allowed in after 4:30pm. Make sure you are in one of the queue lines to enter the *HHN* holding areas: near the Revenge of the Mummy and Finnegan's Bar, in Springfield USA, near TERMINATOR 2: 3-D, and Diagon Alley. Up to four of these waiting areas may be in operation at once. Once you are in line for one of the holding areas, your *HHN* ticket will be scanned and you will be given a wristband.

You will then wait in this holding area. At about 5:45pm, 45 minutes before *HHN* is scheduled to officially begin, you will be allowed into the park again to explore the *HHN* entertainment including the scare houses - usually only a few of them will be open at this time but there will be little or no wait, and you can usually experience them all and then explore the others after 6:30pm when *HHN* officially starts!

Our recommended holding area location is the one near the Revenge of the Mummy and Finnegan's Bar as there is a great atmosphere, and places to sit down, as well as places to grab a bite to eat and a drink. Note that these locations may change in 2016, but the Finnegan's Bar location has been a favorite of ours for years.

Chapter 15

Touring Plans:

In order to make the most of your time at the parks we highly recommend you follow one of our touring plans in this guide. These touring plans are *not* designed in order for you to have a leisurely slow day through the parks, they are designed to get as much accomplished as possible, whilst still having fun.

This may mean crossing the park back and forth in order to save you from being in long queue lines but ultimately it will mean that you can get the most out of your Universal Orlando Resort experience.

Generally speaking, the touring plans will have you doing the most popular attractions (that get the longest wait times) at the start and end of the day when they are least busy; during the middle of the day you will be visiting the attractions which have constant wait times all day, and shows. This enables you to maximize your time.

These touring plans presume you do not have Express Passes. If you do, then you can explore the park in whatever way you want as you won't have to worry about waiting in the queue lines. For the attractions that do not offer Express Pass (notably Harry Potter's *Forbidden Journey* and *Escape from Gringotts*), do these first or last in the day.

It has to be said that at the moment, the Universal Orlando theme parks do not have an abundance of attractions meaning that wait times can be long. It is, however, perfectly possible to do all the rides in a park on the same day with some planning.

We recommend you spend at least one day at each park, and then use a third or fourth day to re-do your favorite attractions at both parks, as well as any others you may have missed.

The key to these touring plans is to arrive at the park well before it opens - that means being at the parking garages at least about 60 minutes before park opening if you are driving in. The parking garages open 90 minutes before official park opening hours. If you want to buy tickets on the day for some reason, then you will need to be at the gates at least 45 minutes before park opening. Otherwise, make sure to be at the park gates at least 30 minutes before opening with your park admission in hand. Park gates regularly open up to 30 minutes before the official stated opening time.

Using this touring plan: If there is a particular attraction you do not wish to experience, simply skip that step and then follow the next one - do not change the order of the steps.

1-Day touring plan for Universal's Islands of Adventure:

Due to the popularity of *The Wizarding World of Harry Potter: Hogsmeade* many guidebooks are recommending you visit this area early in the day - DON'T! This is what everyone is doing, which means that you end up getting yourself into insanely long lines!

The exception to this is if you have Early Entry into *Hogsmeade* – then you should, of course, explore all of Hogsmeade during this first hour, and then follow the touring plan below.

Step 1: Be at the turnstiles with your ticket in hand at least 30 minutes before park opening. Proceed through the gates once they are open. Grab a park map, head straight through the arch and through the *Port of Entry* area of the park. You can come back to explore this beautiful area later in the day.

Step 2: When you reach the end of the path you are forced to turn either left or right. Turn left and cross the bridge under *The Incredible Hulk Coaster*. Turn right and experience *The Amazing Adventures of Spider-Man*. Lockers are not required for this attraction. Do this before riding *The Hulk* because lines for *Spider-Man* build up more quickly, whereas the Hulk's stay constant throughout the day.

Step 3: Walk back to *The Incredible Hulk Coaster* - ride this. Lockers are required for loose items on this ride.

Step 4: Walk back towards *Spider-Man* and ride *Dr. Doom's Fearfall*. Lockers are required for loose items.

Step 5: If all has gone to plan, you should have accomplished all this within the first 45 to 60 minutes of your day.

Step 6: If you are visiting after *Skull Island: Reign of Kong* has opened, this should be your next attraction. Then, follow this plan from step 9 onwards (you can do step 7 and 8 later if you really want to but these are basic kids' rides). If *Kong* is not yet open during your visit, follow the plan from step 7 below as normal.

Step 7: Cross the park to the *Seuss Landing* area. Ride *The Cat in the Hat*. Lockers are not required for this attraction.

Step 8: Ride *Red Fish, Blue Fish, One Fish, Two Fish*. Be prepared to get wet.

Step 9: Now prepare to get absolutely drenched. Head to the *Toon Lagoon* area and hit the three water rides just before lunch. *Dudley's Do-Right's Ripsaw Falls* should be first, followed by *Popeye & Bluto's Bilge-Rat Barges*, and finally *Jurassic Park River Adventure*.

You will be soaking wet before lunch but most people do these rides after lunch, so you have saved yourself a lot of valuable time in the afternoon. We highly advise eating somewhere outdoors, and not inside in the freezing air-conditioning. Alternatively, make sure you have a change of clothes with you and a rent a locker before experiencing the water rides.

Step 10: Have lunch. In the interests of time we recommend that you dine at a quick service location.

Step 11: If you fit the very limited ride requirements, ride *Pteranodon Flyers*. This will most likely be one of the lengthiest waits of the day due to its extremely low capacity.

Step 12: Head to the *Seuss Landing* are and ride the *High in the Sky Seuss Trolley Train Ride*. This ride can also be prone to long waits.

Step 13: Ride the *Caro-seuss-el*. The wait for this should rarely be above 10 minutes.

Step 14: Experience the shows: *Poseidon's* Fury (do not wait more than half an hour for this) and *The Eighth Voyage of Sindbad Stunt Show*. If the *Mystic Fountain* is entertaining guests, enjoy that too.

Step 15: Now you only have a few minor rides left to do, as well as *The Wizarding World of Harry Potter: Hogsmeade*. Here is where you make your decision - if there are three hours until park closing or more, follow the next steps in order. If there are less than 3 hours, you may want to head to *The Wizarding World* and follow this touring plan from step number 19.

Step 16: If *Oh, the Stories You'll Hear* is playing in *Seuss Landing*, then watch this show.

Step 17: Explore the *Camp Jurassic* area near *Pteranodon Flyers*.

Step 18: Ride *Storm Force Accelatron*.

Step 19: Head to *The Wizarding World of Harry Potter: Hogsmeade*. Ride *Dragon Challenge*. The wait for this rarely exceeds 30 minutes. Lockers are required for loose items.

Step 20: Ride *Flight of the Hippogriff*.

Step 21: Have dinner. We recommend *Three Broomsticks* right here in the *Wizarding World*.

Step 22: Experience *Ollivander's Wand Shop*. If you will be going to Universal Studios Florida tomorrow, skip this as they have a clone of this attraction at Diagon Alley but with much shorter wait times.

Step 23: Ride *Harry Potter and the Forbidden Journey*. Lockers are required for loose items. As long as you are in line even one minute before the park closes they will let you experience the ride.

Chances are that within the last hour of the park being open lines for most things throughout the park will be very low and *Forbidden Journey* is often a walk-on at this point of the day with no wait in line.

Top Tip: A common theme park trick is to keep the posted wait times higher than they really are during the last operating hour to trick you into not queuing up for rides. Use your judgment. If the park looks busier now than it did in the middle of the day, it is unlikely there is a 45 or 60 minute wait at a ride at park closing time.

1-Day touring plan for Universal Studios Florida:

Step 1: Be at the turnstiles with your park ticket in hand at least 30 minutes before the schedule park opening time. Proceed through the gates. Grab a park map and head straight ahead towards *Despicable Me* on your left hand side. Ride it. If the wait is longer than 30 minutes, we would recommend you give this ride a miss due to the time you lose here significantly impacting the remainder of your day.

Step 2: Ride *Transformers: The Ride*. There is a single rider line available. If you find that the line for this ride is already very long, then we suggest you skip this step and ride *Transformers* towards the end of the day when queues will be shorter.

Step 3: Ride *Hollywood Rip Ride Rockit*. There is a single rider line available though it is fairly slow moving. At this time of the day, the regular stand by queue line shouldn't be too big anyway. Lockers are required for loose items.

Step 4: Ride *Revenge of the Mummy*. Lockers are required for loose items. A single rider line is available. We highly recommend the regular queue as the single rider line does not move very quickly and you will miss some of the great theming. Wait times for this ride rarely exceed 30 minutes.

Step 5: Ride *The Simpsons Ride*.

Step 6: Ride *Men in Black: Alien Attack*. A single rider line is available. Lockers are required for loose items.

Step 7: Have lunch. We highly recommend you have a Quick Service meal at lunch to maximize your touring time.

Step 8: Watch *Universal's Superstar Parade* if it's the right time. The parade at *Universal Studios Florida* is nowhere near as popular as the parades at Walt Disney World so you should be able to get a front row spot arriving even 10 minutes before the parade starts, especially as the parade route is so long. Often you will even get a front row spot at the parade without stalking out the spot in advance.

Step 9: Ride *E.T. Adventure*. Waits are generally not above 30 minutes.

Step 10: Watch Universal's *Horror Make Up Show*. This is our favorite live show at Universal Orlando Resort. The theatre is fairly small so arrive about 20 minutes before the performance is due to start to be guaranteed a seat.

Step 11: Watch *Terminator 2: 3D...A Battle Across Time*. This is our other favorite live show at Universal Orlando Resort, and is very different to the *Horror Make Up Show*.

Step 12: Head to *The Wizarding World of Harry Potter: Diagon Alley*. You will want to enter this area *at least* 3 hours before park closing for the full experience. Crowds will be lowest at the end of the day. Ride *Harry Potter and the Escape from Gringotts*, followed by a return journey on the *Hogwarts Express* (note a Park-to-Park ticket is required for access to the Hogwarts Express). If you have time, experience the *Ollivander's* wand shop/show.

Step 13: Watch the *Universal Cinematic Spectacular*. Views are available from all around the lagoon but in front of TRANSFORMERS is a good spot. We would not be too worried about missing the *Cinematic Spectacular* to get entry into *Diagon Alley* and experience its attractions.

Important Note: This touring plan does not include all attractions in the park due to time constraints. Some attractions target younger children such as *Barney* and *Woody Woodpecker* that may not be suitable for your party. If you have no interest in *The Wizarding World of Harry Potter* it is feasible to do almost all the *other* attractions in this park in a day with careful planning.

Best of both parks 1-day touring plan.

In this touring plan we will detail how to hit the biggest attractions in both parks. It is *not* feasible to do all attractions at the two parks in just one day, so we have listed the must-dos here. Remember you will need a Universal Orlando Park-to-Park ticket to access both parks on the same day. Doing the best of both parks in one day has become much more difficult since the addition of *The Wizarding World of Harry Potter: Diagon Alley* and its rides, due to its immense popularity and the extra guests this has brought to the Universal Orlando Resort.

On extremely busy days, it is unlikely that you will be able to accomplish everything in this plan. This touring plan assumes high crowds and the parks are open until at least 9:00pm. The plan can also work for lower crowds and shorter opening times.

Step 1: Be at the turnstiles of *Universal Studios Florida* with your ticket in hand before park opening. Be there at least 30 minutes before the park is set to open, as queues build quickly. Proceed through the turnstiles, grab a park map and head straight ahead towards *Despicable Me* on your left hand side. Ride it.

Step 2: Ride *Transformers: The Ride*. Use the single rider line to save time if you can.

Step 3: Ride *Hollywood Rip Ride Rockit*. Use the single rider line to save time if you can. You have now ridden three of the rides with the longest waits in this park.

Step 4: Now be prepared to walk all the way across the park. Ride *The Simpsons Ride*.

Step 5: If it is past 12:30pm at this point, skip this step. Otherwise, Ride *MEN IN BLACK: Alien Attack*.

Step 6: Ride *Revenge of the Mummy*.

Step 7: If it is past 1:45pm at this point, skip this step. Otherwise, Watch the fantastic *Universal Horror Make-Up Show*. Work this around your lunch so either watch it before or after lunch - try to be there 20 minutes early.

Step 8: Lunch - we recommend *Monsters' Cafe* if you are staying in *Universal Studios Florida* and want a quick meal. Having a table service meal will seriously impede your ability to see the most of both parks in a day.

Step 9: Now it is time for the long walk as you make your way over to the other theme park - *Universal's Islands of Adventure*. Be prepared for long queue lines as this is the busiest point in the day - however lines will still generally be shorter than at *Universal Studios Florida*, which is why we started there first.

Step 10: Ride *The Incredible Hulk Coaster*. There is a single-rider line available.

Step 11: If it is past 4:00pm we recommend you skip this step. Otherwise, choose one of the following water attractions. Ride *Dudley Do-Right's Ripsaw Falls*, *Popeye & Bluto's Bilge-Rat Barges* or *Jurassic Park River Adventure*.

Step 12: Ride *The Amazing Adventures of Spider-Man*. The queue will be long at this time of day. Use the single rider line if possible to save time.

Step 13: Explore *The Wizarding World of Harry Potter: Hogsmeade*. The crowds will probably have lightened by now. Ride *Dragon Challenge*, which should not have a wait longer than 30 minutes, especially at this point in the day.

Step 14: Ride *Harry Potter and the Forbidden Journey*. The line should be substantially smaller than it is in the morning.

Step 15: Catch the *Hogwarts Express* over to *Diagon Alley*. If you are boarding the train 30 minutes or sooner before the park officially closes you will have to move quickly to make it to the final ride.

Step 16: Proceed to *Escape from Gringotts*. This ride may have a long queue, but it should be at the lowest it has been all day. As long as you are in the queue line before park closing you will be able to ride, except in periods of extremely high crowds where the queue line may be closed earlier. If time still remains, have dinner somewhere in the *Wizarding World* or elsewhere in the park.

Note: For those staying at on-site hotels, do step 16 then step 15 first at *Universal Studios Florida* using your Early Access privilege and be there before park opening. Then pick up the plan from Step 1 and *Despicable Me*.

Chapter 16

The Future:

The future of the Universal Orlando Resort is looking bright with several projects currently in the works. In this section we cover what will be coming soon to the resort, including the theme parks, and what you can look forward to.

In September 2013 Universal's President and Chief Executive Officer, Steve Burke, announced at a conference in California that they plan to open one new attraction per year for the foreseeable future. This is a pace that no other major theme park resort can match, and sets an exciting precedent for the future of the resort.

Sapphire Falls Resort – Confirmed (Summer 2016):

A new resort hotel will be coming to the Universal Orlando Resort in Summer 2016, bringing the total number of on-site hotels to five. Guests visiting the new Loews Sapphire Falls Resort at Universal Orlando will walk into a colorful Caribbean hideaway built around a lush, tropical lagoon and towering waterfall. Its 1,000 rooms, including 77 suites, will bring the number of on-site hotel rooms at the Universal Orlando resort to 5,200.

A resort-style pool with a water slide, children's play area, sand beach and fire pit will form a central courtyard that will be surrounded by the hotel's guest rooms. There will be water taxi and shuttle access to all of the entertainment and dining options throughout Universal Orlando Resort.

Amenities will include Early Park Admission to Universal Orlando's theme parks, a full-service restaurant with scenic views and outdoor dining, a themed lobby lounge, poolside bar and grill, quick-service marketplace, valet service and a fitness center.

This hotel will *not* include complimentary Universal Express Pass unlimited access.

King Kong Attraction – Confirmed (Summer 2016):

A King Kong attraction has long been rumored for *Islands of Adventure* but now its really happening – and it is opening this summer at the Universal Orlando Resort. *Skull Island: Reign of Kong* will be a multi-sensory, multi-dimensional new ride where passengers will board 4x4 vehicles. The ride will turn into a "fight for survival as you encounter creatures of unknown origin and even the great Kong himself".

The façade of the ride building is immense and we are very excited for this new addition to *Islands of Adventure*.

Volcano Bay Water Park – Confirmed (2017):

Universal Orlando Resort has ambitious plans to expand its offerings, and rival the Walt Disney World resort, which is only a few miles away. One of the ways it is doing this, is by building an incredibly highly-themed water park.

Although Universal already owns the land on which Wet 'n Wild sits, it does not have its own on-site water park with integrated tickets, room charging and other facilities. Wet 'n' Wild will also be closing at the end of 2016, meaning that the new water park – Volcano Bay – will replace it.

The park will measure in at about 30 acres which is comparable to the size of Wet 'n Wild, and half of the size of one of the Walt Disney World water parks. The park is expected to being built on a plot of land south of the Cabana Bay Beach Resort, with the central icon being a "massive, 200-foot erupting volcano".

Universal Orlando says this water park will feature "radically-innovative attractions, peaceful moments of relaxation and an experience that we hope will change the way guests think about water theme parks."

No exact opening date has been given so far the park, except 2017. It would be logical, however, to have it open in time for the busy summer period.

Fast and Furious Ride – Confirmed (2017):

A new *Fast & Furious: Supercharged* attraction will be making its way to Universal Studios Florida in 2017. This attraction will be located in the San Francisco area of the park, and the two previous attractions in this are – *Beetlejuice* and *Disaster*, have now closed to make way for construction of this new ride.

Universal says: "This ride is going to fuse everything you love about the films with an original storyline and incredible ride technology. You'll get to check out some of the high-speed, supercharged cars you've seen on the big screen. You'll be immersed in the underground racing world made famous in the films and explore the headquarters of Toretto and his team. Then, you'll board specially-designed vehicles for an adrenaline-pumping ride with your favorite stars from the films."

We expect this new attraction to be similar to the Fast & Furious attraction at Universal Hollywood, which consists of a giant tram filled with guests and a wraparound 3D screen which shows a chase sequence as your tram moves in time with it.

Cabana Bay Beach Resort Expansion – Confirmed (2017):

Universal Orlando has announced that their prime value resort – Cabana Bay – has proved so popular that they are going to expand it. This will allow more guests to stay on-site at Universal Orlando at their most affordable rooms.

The expansion will add 400 guest rooms in two new towers. Some of these rooms will have amazing views of Universal's Volcano Bay water park.

Jimmy Fallon Attraction – Confirmed (2017):

In what is a piece of bizarre news, a new attraction called "Race Through New York Starring Jimmy Fallon" will be coming to Universal Studios Florida in 2017. This attraction is replacing 'Twister' which has now shut down.

Universal says: "Inspired by the popular Tonight Show segment, this upcoming ride "Race through New York Starring Jimmy Fallon" will pit you against Jimmy in a wild race through one of the world's greatest cities – New York City. Opens in 2017. Guests step right into Studio 6B where Jimmy will challenge them. On the adventure, they will twist, turn and laugh as they speed through the streets – and skies – of The Big Apple – encountering everything from iconic landmarks to the deepest subway tunnels – and anything else that comes to Jimmy's mind."

New Nintendo attractions coming – Confirmed:

In May 2015, Universal Parks and Resorts announced a partnership with Nintendo. A Universal Orlando press release says that "Together, these two storytelling giants will create spectacular, dedicated experiences based on Nintendo's wildly popular games, characters and worlds… The immersive experiences will include major attractions at Universal's theme parks and will feature Nintendo's most famous characters and games."

No specific details have been given on the franchises that will be coming to the resort but we are excited for the possibilities.

And more...

Universal Orlando also plans to more than triple the number of onsite hotel rooms to between 10,000 and 15,000 in the future. With a new water park coming and new attractions, they could certainly do with more on-site rooms.

Chapter 17
Park Maps:

Universal Studios Florida Attractions

PRODUCTION CENTRAL
1   Despicable Me Minion Mayhem (Express)
2   Shrek 4-D (Express)
3   Hollywood Rip Ride Rockit (Express)
4   TRANSFORMERS: The Ride-3D (Express)
5   Music Plaza Stage

NEW YORK
6   Revenge of the Mummy (Express)
7   The Blues Brothers Show

THE WIZARDING WORLD OF HARRY POTTER- DIAGON ALLEY™
8   The Knight Bus
9   Hogwarts Express - King's Cross Station
10 Knockturn Alley
11 Ollivanders
12 Harry Potter and the Escape from Gringotts
13 Live Performances

WORLD EXPO
14 Fear Factor Live (Express)
15 MEN IN BLACK Alien Attack (Express)
16 The Simpsons Ride (Express)
17 Kang & Kodos' Twirl 'n' Hurl

WOODY WOODPECKER'S KIDZONE'
18 Animal Actor's on Location! (Express)
19 A Day in the Park with Barney (Express)
20 Curious George Goes To Town
21 Woody Woodpecker's Nuthouse Coaster (Express)
22 Fievel's Playland
23 E.T. Adventure (Express)

HOLLYWOOD
24 Universal Orlando's Horror Make-Up Show (Express)
25 TERMINATOR 2: 3-D (Express)

PARADE ROUTE
26 Universal's Superstar Parade

PARK-WIDE ENTERTAINMENT
27 Universal's Cinematic Spectacular: 100 Years of Movie Memories

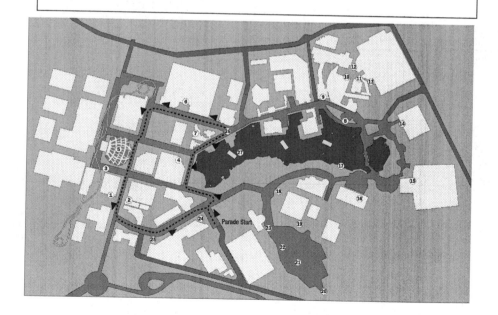

Islands of Adventure Attractions

MARVEL SUPER HERO ISLAND
1 The Incredible Hulk Coaster - Express
2 Storm Force Accelatron - Express
3 Doctor Doom's Fearfall - Express
4 The Amazing Adventures of Spider-Man - Express

TOON LAGOON
5 Me Ship, The Olive
6 Popeye & Bluto's Bilge-Rat Barges - Express
7 Dudley Do-Right's Ripsaw Falls - Express

JURASSIC PARK
8 Pteranodon Flyers
9 Camp Jurassic
10 Jurassic Park River Adventure - Express
11 Skull Island - Reign of Kong
12 Jurassic Park Discovery Center

THE WIZARDING WORLD OF HARRY POTTER™ - HOGSMEADE
13 Harry Potter and the Forbidden Journey
14 Flight of the Hippogriff - Express
15 Live Performances
16 Ollivanders
17 Dragon Challenge - Express
18 Hogwarts Express - Hogsmeade Station

THE LOST CONTINENT
19 The Eighth Voyage of Sindbad Stunt Show - Express
20 The Mystic Fountain
21 Poseidon's Fury - Express

SEUSS LANDING
22 The High in the Sky Seuss Trolley Train Ride! - Express
23 Caro-Seuss-el - Express
24 One Fish, Two Fish, Red Fish, Blue Fish - Express
25 The Cat In The Hat - Express
26 If I Ran The Zoo

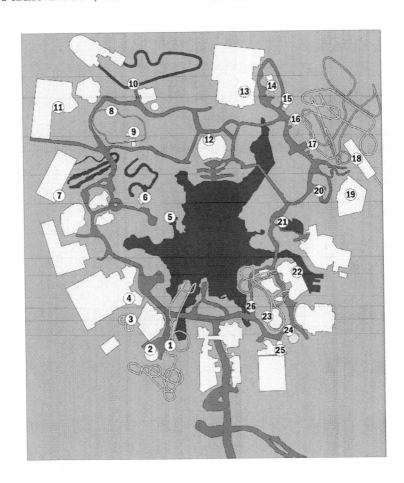

Chapter 18

A Special Thanks:

If you have made it this far, thank you very much for reading everything – we hope this guide has made a big difference to your vacation and you have found some tips that will save you time, money and hassle! Remember to take this guide with you whilst you are on vacation.

To get in touch, please use the 'Contact Us' form on our website at **http://www.independentguidebooks.com/contact-us/**. If you have any corrections, feedback about any element of the guide, or a review of a ride or restaurant, send us a message and we will get back to you! You could even help contribute to the ride and show reviews we will be including in future editions of this guide.

To stay up to date on all the latest developments and updates be sure to like our Facebook page at **http://www.facebook.com/independentguidebooks/** and on Twitter at **http:///www.twitter.com/indepguide**. You can also sign up to our newsletter on our website (on the right sidebar) at **http://www.independentguidebooks.com**.

If you have enjoyed this guide you will want to check out:
The Independent Guide to Walt Disney World
The Independent Guide to Orlando
The Independent Guide to Disneyland
The Independent Guide to Disneyland Paris
The Independent Guide to Paris

All guides are available right now in both digital and print formats!

Our theme park guide books give you detailed information on every ride, show and attraction and more insider tips that will save you hours in line! Our city guides are great overviews of the cities with top attractions, good places to eat and stay, explanations of the transport system and much more.

All that's left to say is: have fun at the Universal Orlando Resort!

Photo credits:
The following photos have been used in this guide under a **Creative Commons attribution 2.0 license**.

Thank you to: *Chad Sparkes* for Gringotts; *Jared* for Knockturn alley and London waterfront; *Jeremy Thompson* for Blue Man Group, Popeye & Bluto's Bilge-Rat Barges, Pteranodon Flyers, Terminator 2: 3D, Woody Woodpecker's Nuthouse Coaster, Caro-seuss-el, Jurassic Park River Adventure, Jurassic Park Discovery Center, The Amazing Adventures of Spider-Man, Rip Ride Rockit (cover) and Animal Actors on Location; *Joe Shlabotnik* for Universal CityWalk; *Katy Warner* for the photo of the Hard Rock Hotel; *LancerE* for AMC cinemas; *Rhonda Oglesby* for Hogwart's Express; *Martin Lewison* - Cat in the Hat; *Ross Hawkes* for One fish, two fish; *Shawn Rossi* for the photo of Royal Pacific Resort; *Stan Shebs* for the photo of Loews Portofino Bay Hotel; *Steve Fishman* for the picture of the Universal globe; *Steve Straitor* for Transformers; *Universal Orlando Resort* for Cabana Bay Beach Resort, Portofino Bay Hotel, and Escape from Gringotts; *Walter* for Men in Black;

29576681R00091

Made in the USA
Middletown, DE
24 February 2016